EIGHTEENTH CENTURY NORTH CAROLINA IMPRINTS

EIGHTEENTH CENTURY
NORTH CAROLINA
IMPRINTS
1749-1800
By DOUGLAS C. McMURTRIE

Chapel Hill
The University of North Carolina Press
1938

TO
MARY THORNTON
CONSERVATOR OF MATERIALS FOR
NORTH CAROLINA HISTORY
THIS VOLUME IS
APPRECIATIVELY INSCRIBED

ILLUSTRATIONS

The Journal of the House of Burgesses, . . . North-Carolina. New Bern, James Davis, 1749. From the Public Record Office copy (reduced) 29

A Collection of All the Public Acts of Assembly. New Bern, James Davis, 1751. From the New York Public Library copy (reduced) 31

The Journal of the House of Burgesses. New Bern, James Davis, 1754. From the Public Record Office copy (reduced) 35

Draught of an Act . . . for Establishing a Paper Credit. New Bern, James Davis, 1754. From the Public Record Office copy (reduced) 39

Sermon . . . December the 27th, 1755, . . . By Michael Smith, A.B. New Bern, James Davis, 1756. From the Historical Society of Pennsylvania copy 43

Broadside proclamation by Governor Arthur Dobbs, April 29, 1758. From the Public Record Office copy (reduced) 45

The Validity of Infant Baptism. New Bern, James
   Davis, 1758. From the Massachusetts Historical Society copy 49
Laws of North Carolina, 1764. Wilmington, Andrew
   Steuart, 1764. From the University of North Carolina
   copy (reduced) 57
Laws of North Carolina, 1765. Wilmington, Andrew
   Steuart, 1765. From copy in the Moravian Archives,
   Winston-Salem, N. C. 61
On the Important Duty of Subjection to the Civil Powers.
   New Bern, James Davis, 1768. From the Public Record Office copy 63
A Complete Revisal of All the Acts of Assembly. New
   Bern, James Davis, 1773. From the University of
   North Carolina copy 71
The Office and Authority of a Justice of the Peace. New
   Bern, James Davis, 1774. From the copy of Mr. Bruce
   Cotten 73
*At a General Meeting of the Inhabitants of the District
   of Wilmington . . . July 21st, 1774.* [Wilmington, Adam Boyd, 1774.] From the Public Record Office copy (reduced) 77
*At a Meeting of the Committee for the County of Craven,
   . . . 4th Day of March, 1775.* [New Bern, 1775.]
   From the Public Record Office copy (reduced) . . 79
*The Journal of the . . . Provincial Congress of
   North-Carolina.* New Bern, James Davis, 1775. From
   the Public Record Office copy 81
Broadside with the imprint of Robert Keith, New Bern,
   1783. From the Library of Congress copy (reduced) 97
*Proceedings and Debates of the Convention of North-
   Carolina.* Edenton, Hodge & Wills, 1789. From the
   New York Public Library copy 111

[vi]

The Ratification of the Constitution of the United States, by . . . North-Carolina. [Edenton, Hodge & Wills, 1789.] From the New York Public Library copy   113

Journal of the Convention of . . . North-Carolina. [Edenton, Hodge & Wills, 1789.] From the North Carolina Historical Commission copy 115

The Bible Defended. Halifax, Abraham Hodge, 1797. From the Presbyterian Historical Society copy . . . 151

Hodge's North-Carolina Almanack, for . . . 1799. Halifax, Abraham Hodge, 1798. From the copy of Mr. Bruce Cotten 153

An Eulogium, . . . Death of General George Washington, Salisbury, Francis Coupee, 1800. From the New York Public Library copy 167

An oration on the Death of General George Washington. Raleigh, Joseph Gales, 1800. From the New York Public Library copy 169

INTRODUCTION

As is well known, printing was introduced into North Carolina in 1749, in which year James Davis set up a press at New Bern. In 1740, the House of Burgesses had had its proceedings printed at Williamsburg, Va., where a permanent press had been established ten years earlier. In 1745, John Hodgson had offered in the assembly a bill to "Enable and Encourage the persons hereinafter mentioned to print the Laws of this Province," but the bill appears to have failed of passage, and we have no clue to the identity of the persons referred to.

The revisal and printing of the laws was agitated many a time and oft, without tangible result. As early as 1736, Governor Johnston called the matter to the attention of the assembly, and again in 1739, and still again in 1740. Once more, in 1744, he reminded the assembly of "the shameful condition" of their laws.

In 1746, the assembly, roused to the necessity for action, passed an act appointing commissioners to "Revise and Print the Laws of this Province, and for granting to his Majesty, for defraying the Charge thereof, a Duty on Wine, Rum and distilled Liquors and Rice imported into this Province." It was pointed out that "for want of the Laws of this Province being revised and printed, the Magistrates are often at a loss how to discharge their Duty, and the People transgress many of them through want of knowing the same."

The commissioners appointed were Edward Moseley, Samuel Swann, Enoch Hall, and Thomas Barker. Such of them as actually made the revisal were to receive sixty pounds proclamation money, and they were allowed one hundred pounds more for printing, furnishing, and delivering the books. They were not to charge more than twenty shillings a volume, but were to have the sole right of selling the laws for five years.

The revisal was completed, almost wholly by the hand of Swann, and laid before the assembly in 1749 for final approval. As the editorial work approached completion, it was evident the province would need a printer. James Davis, who it is thought had been working in the office of William Parks at Williamsburg, was induced to move to New Bern, to execute the public printing of North Carolina.

The bill for the "encouragement" of Davis was introduced in the assembly on April 6, 1749, by Rufus Marsden. After the customary three readings in both the House and the Council, the bill was finally passed on April 10 and approved by the Governor on April 14.

By the terms of this act James Davis was to be paid for five years a yearly salary of one hundred and sixty pounds, proclamation money. For this salary, Davis was required to reside in New Bern "and to print, with the same Type or Letter with which his Petition now laid before this House, is printed on ... " I interrupt the quotation here to call attention to this mention of a printed petition, an imprint which would be of the greatest interest, could it be brought to light. Undoubtedly this petition was printed in Virginia for, at the time, Davis had not yet brought a press to North Carolina.

To resume the quotation, Davis was to print, "at every Session of Assembly in this Province, the Speeches and addresses at the

Opening of each Session; also the Journals and Proceedings of the House of Burgesses and Deliver Copies thereto [thereof] to each Member who shall attend at such Session; and shall also, as soon as the same can or may be done, print all such Laws as shall be passed at each Sessions, and shall transmit One Copy of them to his excellency, the Governor, and one to each Member of his Majesty's Honourable Council, and also one copy to each Member of the General Assembly in the several Counties in this Province; one copy to each of the Clerks of the House of Assembly, for the use of the said Assembly; one Copy to the Clerk of the General Court, for the use of the said Court; one Copy to the Clerk of each respective County Court in this Province, for the use of such Court; and also one Copy for each and every Justice of the several Counties in this Province, not exceeding Twelve Copies to be sent to the said Justices of any one County; and supply such Copies of the said Journals and Laws as shall or may be necessary, to be transmitted from this Province to the Board of Offices in England, as usual; and also, shall print, and transmit to the Proper Places, the Public Proclamations, and all other Acts of Government."

The printer's salary was to be raised by levy of a tax of four pence, proclamation money, for five years, "on each and every Taxable Person within this Province."

The actual term of Davis's employment began on June 25, 1749, as we learn from a resolution of the Assembly on October 17 approving advance payment of the first half-year's salary of eighty pounds which was to become due "the Twenty fifth day of December next." Payment was not "for stamping and emitting £21350 public bills of credit," as stated by Weeks, for certainly the printer did not "emit" currency. As I read the record, he was to be paid "by the commissioners for stamping and emitting the sum of Twenty One Thousand Three Hundred and Fifty Pounds public Bills of Credit" — in other words, by the fiscal agency of the government. During the period Davis had undoubtedly done many pieces of printing, though he may have printed the paper money as well. In 1754, the employment of James Davis as printer to the province was extended, and again in 1757, and still again in 1760. For many years thereafter he served North Carolina as its official typographer.

This brief introduction to a bibliography does not aim to present a history of early printing in North Carolina. I have endeavored to summarize the present state of knowledge on that subject in the North Carolina chapter in Volume 11 of my *History of Printing in the United States,* published in 1936.

Stephen B. Weeks has provided us with the best previous study of the early North Carolina press. In 1891 was published his *Press of North Carolina in the Eighteenth Century,* to which was appended a bibliography of eighteenth century North Carolina imprints. A list of supplementary titles was included in his "Libraries and Literature in North Carolina in the Eighteenth Century" which appeared in the *Annual Report of the American Historical Association for 1895,* p. 171-267. In these two contributions, Weeks lists 139 imprints, 76 of which were located and thus definitely known and accessible, and 63 not located and therefore, to a considerable extent, in the realm of conjecture.

Of these 63 unlocated titles I have been able in the present list to locate 39. Of the 24 remaining titles, 17 remain unlocated, and I have excluded from my list one (Weeks No. 71) because it was printed by James Adams at Wilmington, Delaware, rather than in North Carolina, and six others (Weeks Nos. 36, 41, 77, 119, 129 and 130) because the evidence of their actual issue seemed to me insufficient.

In the present bibliography are recorded 290 titles, all but 53 of which are located. The 237 located titles more than triples the 76 imprints located by Weeks. In making this comparison I wish emphatically to disclaim any thought critical of Dr. Weeks' pioneer work, done nearly fifty years ago, and for which I have the heartiest respect.

Charles Evans, in his *American Bibliography,* listed all the North Carolina titles which came to his attention. Since he did not have the opportunity of doing intensive work in this field, however, the number of North Carolina titles in his monumental work are comparatively few.

In any bibliography dealing with material of historical interest, the location of titles is all-important. Every effort has been made, therefore, to locate copies of the books and pamphlets known to have been printed in North Carolina earlier than 1801, and some degree of success has attended this effort, as will appear from the figures already given.

There are unfortunate breaks in the colonial session laws, for those of but twenty sessions between 1751 and 1775 are found in contemporary printed form. It is likely that the laws for the missing years were printed at the time, but that copies have not been preserved to us.

The original printed journals for only nine sessions during this period have been found, though those for a number of other sessions are known to have been printed.

For the period of statehood, copies of session laws for all sessions before 1801 have been found and recorded. For a little over half of these sessions have printed legislative journals been located, though many of those for the missing sessions must have been printed.

The subjoined tables of the eighteenth century legislative sessions of both colony and state during the period here dealt with show (by an x) those for which printed journals and session laws have been found.

COLONIAL PERIOD

Session and Dates of Sitting		Assembly Journals Colonial Records	Laws Colonial Records	
7th	1749: Sep. 26 — Oct. 18	4: 1010-1027	x	*
8th	1750: Mar. 28 — Apr. 9	4: 1051-1064†		*
9th	1750: July 5 — July 10	4: 1068-1073	x 23: 349-351	*

* Published in the *Collection of All the Public Acts of Assembly,* 1751.
† Journal of the Council only.

COLONIAL PERIOD

	Session and Dates of Sitting	Assembly Journals Colonial Records		Laws Colonial Records	
10th	1751: Sep. 26 — Oct. 12	4: 1274-1300	x	23: 352-370	
				25: 243-247	x
11th	1752: Mar. 31 — Apr. 15	4: 1329-1348	x	23: 371-386	x
				25: 248-249	x
12th	1753: Mar. 28 — Apr. 12	5: 53-77	x	23: 387-391	x
12th	1753: Mar. 28 — Apr. 12	5: 53-77	x	23: 387-391	x
				25: 250-256	x
13th	1754: Feb. 19 — Mar. 9	5: 191-212	x	23: 392-399	x
				25: 257-273	x
				23: 401-421	
1st	1754: Dec. 12 — 1755: Jan. 15	5: 231-262; 281-312‡		25: 274-312	x
2nd	1755: Sep. 25 — Oct. 15	5: 520-559		23: 422-439	
				25: 313-330	x
3rd	1756: Sep. 30 — Oct. 26	5: 688-738		23: 440-474	
				25: 331-344	x
4th	1757: May 16 — May 28	5: 843-868		23: 475	
				25: 345-349	x
5th	1757: Nov. 21 — Dec. 14	5: 889-925		23: 476-482	
				25: 350-360	x
6th	1758: Apr. 28 — May 4	5: 998-1012		23: 483-484	
				25: 361-369	x
7th	1758: Nov. 23 — Dec. 23	5: 1039-1101		23: 485-501	
				25: 370-390	x
8th	1759: May 8 — May 18	6: 95-114		23: 502	
				25: 391-392	x
9th	1759: Nov. 23 — 1760: Jan. 9	6: 132-171; 184-		23: 503-509	
				25: 393-404	x
1st	1760: Apr. 24 — May 23	6: 362-420		23: 510-514	
				25: 405-432	x
2nd	1760: May 26 — May 27	6: 427-446		23: 515	
				25: 433-449	x
3rd	1760: June 30 — July 14	6: 438-446†		23: 516-522	x
4th	1760: Nov. 7 — Dec. 3	6: 469-511		23: 523-538	
				25: 450-456	
5th	1760: Dec. 5 — Dec. 6	6: 513-520		No laws	
1st	1761: Mar. 31 — Apr. 23	6: 661-697		23: 539-549	
				25: 457-467	
1st	1762: Apr. 13 — Apr. 29	6: 800-837	x	No laws	
1st	1762: Nov. 3 — Dec. 11	6: 893-965		23: 550-595	
				25: 468-482	x
1st	1764: Feb. 3 — Mar. 10	6: 1150-1218		23: 596-631	
				25: 483-485	**

† Journal of the Council only.
‡ The printed journal (no. 17) contains the proceedings through December 23, 1754.
** The laws of this session seem to have been printed only in the *Collection of All the Acts of Assembly*, 1764 (no. 45), p. 309-386.

COLONIAL PERIOD

	Session and Dates of Sitting	Assembly Journals Colonial Records	Laws Colonial Records	
2nd	1764: Oct. 25 — Nov. 28	6: 1257-1318	23: 632-659	
			25: 486-490	††
3rd	1765: May 3 — May 18	7: 61-88	23: 660-663	x
1st	1766: Nov. 3 — Dec. 2	7: 342-423	23: 664-687	
			25: 494-509	x
2nd	1767: Dec. 5 — 1768: Jan. 16	7: 565-594; 624-670	23: 688-758	
			25: 510-513	
3rd	1768: Nov. 7 — Dec. 5	7: 924-986	23: 759-783	
			25: 514-517	
1st	1769: Oct. 23 — Nov. 6	8: 105-141	23: 784-786	
			25: 518-519	
1st	1770: Dec. 5 — 1771: Jan. 26	8: 302-346; 385-479 x	23: 787-849	
			25: 519a-519f	
2nd	1771: Nov. 19 — Dec. 23	9: 136-225	23: 850-871	
			25: 520-522	
1st	1773: Jan. 25 — Mar. 6	9: 447-591	23: 872-930	
1st	1773: Dec. 4 — Dec. 21	9: 773-788	No laws	
2nd	1774: Mar. 2 — Mar. 25	9: 874-953	23: 931-976	x
	1775: Apr. 4 — Apr. 6	9: 1187-1205	No laws	

†† Printed separately by Andrew Steuart (no. 44) and also included by Davis in his 1764 *Collection of All the Acts.*

AFTER STATEHOOD

	Session and Dates of Sitting	Journals State Records	H	S	Laws
1	1777: Apr. 8 — May 9	12: 1-113			x
2	1777: Nov. 15 — Dec. 24	12: 265-452			x
1	1778: Apr. 14 — May 1?	12: 665-764	x	x	x
2	1778: Aug. 8 — Aug. 19	12: 816-879	x	x	x
3	1779: Jan. 19 — Feb. 12?	13: 625-734			x
1	1779: May 3 — May 15	13: 784-824			
		18: 803-825	x		x
2	1779: Oct. 18 — Nov. 10?	13: 913-1000			x
1	1780: Apr. 17 — May 10?	MS*			x
2	1780: Sep. 5 — Sep. 13?	MS*			
3	1781: Jan. 18 — Feb. 14	H 17: 715-793*			
		S 635-714			x
1	1781: June 23 — July 14	S 17: 794-876†			x
		H : 877-978‡			
1	1782: Apr. 13 — May 12	S 19: 1-128			
		H 16: 1-177*			x
1	1783: Apr. 18 — May 17	S 19: 129-232			
		H : 233-368‡	x		x
1	1784: Apr. 19 — June 3	S			

AFTER STATEHOOD

	Session and Dates of Sitting	Journals State Records	H	S	Laws
		H 19: 489-716	x	x	x
1	1784: Oct. 22 — Nov. 26	S 19: 400-488			
		H : 717-836‡			x
1	1785: Nov. 19 — Dec. 29	S			
		H 17: 264-426*	x	x	x
1	1786: Nov. 18 — 1787: Jan. 6				
1	1787: Nov. 19 — Dec. 22*				
1	1788: Nov. 3 — Dec. 6				
1	1789: Nov. 2 — Dec. 22				
1	1790: Nov. 1 — Dec. 15				
1	1791: Dec. 5 — 1792: Jan. 20				
1	1792: Nov. 15 — 1793: Jan. 1				
1	1793: Dec. 2 — 1794: Jan. 11				
2	1794: July 7 — July 19*				
1	1794: Dec. 30 — 1795: Feb. 7				
1	1795: Nov. 2 — Dec. 9				
1	1796: Nov. 21 — Dec. 24?				
1	1797: Nov. 20 — Dec. 23				
1	1798: Nov. 19 — Dec. 29?				
1	1799: Nov. 18 — Dec. 23				
1	1800: Nov. 17 — Dec. 20				

Of all the sessions following 1785, printed journals of both senate and house, and printed session laws, are recorded in the bibliography.

* Recorded as "MS, State Archives" in "Colonial Assemblies and Their Journals," *American Historical Association Annual Report for 1897*, p. 440-441.
† Incomplete.
‡ Recorded as "Journal wanting" in "Colonial Assemblies and their Journals," *loc. cit.*

Many more unlocated titles could have been added to this bibliography, had it been decided to include titles for journals and session laws now missing. Titles of the following have been included, although no printed copies of them have been found. included, although no printed copies of them have been found (printed laws have been located for the sessions marked*):

    Laws   November-December 1760 (Weeks No. 22)
    Journal November-December 1762 (Weeks No. 24)
    Journal February-March   1764 (Weeks No. 27)
    Journal May   1765 (Weeks No. 30)

On the other hand, a long series of laws and journals, which Weeks does not happen to mention, have *not* been included:

Colonial Period:
    Journal: March-April 1750*

September-October 1755*
September-October 1756*
May 1757*
November-December 1757*
April-May 1758*
November-December 1758*
May 1759*
November 1759 — January 1760*
April-May 1760*
May 1760*
June-July 1760*

Journal, November-December 1760 (Weeks No. 22 records the Laws only)
Journal and Laws, March-April 1761
Journal, October-November 1764*
Journal, November-December 1766*
Journal and Laws: December 1767 — January 1768
                November-December 1768
Laws   October-November 1769 (printed Journal located)
                December 1770 — January 1771 (printed Journal located)
Journal and Laws: November-December 1771
Laws   January-March 1773 (printed Journal located)
Journal and Laws, April 1775 (4-day session; perhaps there were none)

Period of Statehood (Laws of all sessions located):
Journals,   April-May 1777
               November-December 1777
Senate Journal, April 1778 (printed House journal located)
Senate Journal, August 1778 (printed House journal located)
Journals,   January-February 1779
Senate Journal, May 1779 (printed House journal located)

Journals: October-November 1779
              April-May 1780 ("MS, State Archives")
              September 1780 ("MS, State Archives")
              January-February 1781 ("MS, State Archives")
              June-July 1781 ("Wanting")
              April-May 1782 ("MS, State Archives")
Senate Journal, April-May 1783 (printed House journal located)
Journals,   October-November 1784 ("Wanting")

Although titles for the above have not been included in the bibliography, there is clear evidence that many of them were printed and a reasonable presumption that most if not all of them were issued in printed form. For instance, though some of the printed journals of the general assembly for the years 1778-1780 cannot now be found, we have a long memorial of Davis to the assembly in 1780 on the difficulties of the printer's work under war conditions, in which he says "He now begs leave to acquaint the general assembly that he has served them two years [since his last appointment in April, 1778]; has printed and published the Laws and Journals of four sessions . . . and has not received more than 20 or 30 pounds of real value."[1]

At the end of this volume will be found a supplement listing doubtful imprints, the evidence of whose existence was not thought sufficient to justify their inclusion in the bibliography. Some of these may turn up some time; some, of course, may never have been printed.

It is not claimed that every extant copy of titles in the list of imprints has been recorded, although a quite diligent effort has been made to ascertain what was to be found in the principal libraries, especially those of North Carolina, and in a number of highly specialized libraries elsewhere, such as the Baptist and Masonic collections.

[1] *North Carolina State Records,* xx, 224.

Of the titles listed, the most widely distributed in copies still extant seems to be Iredell's revisal of the laws, 1791 (no. 170), of which 29 copies have been located in 24 collections. Also of wide distribution are nos. 180 (19 copies in 18 libraries), 69 (16 copies), 199 (14 copies), 182 (13 copies), 144 and 265 (11 copies of each). Ten copies have been recorded of nos. 7, 166, and 213.

A rather surprising total of 108 titles are known from single copies only. This total includes 38 issues of the earlier laws and journals and certain Revolutionary documents, all of which I have been able to find only in the Public Record Office, London. Of the remaining 70 titles recorded from single copies, 15 are in the library of the University of North Carolina and 13 (one of which is "lost") are recorded from the Library of Congress. The New York Public Library has 8 of these "singletons," the John Carter Brown Library has 5, the Supreme Court Library at Raleigh, the Duke University Library, and the Historical Society of Pennsylvania have 3 each. The Henry E. Huntington Library and the Harvard Law School Library have 2 each, and one apiece can be found in the Supreme Council Library, Washington, the Congregational Library, Boston, the Harvard College Library, the Massachusetts Historical Society, the American Antiquarian Society, the New York Masonic Grand Lodge Library, the Sondley Library of Asheville, the Wake Forest College Library, the American Baptist Historical Society, the Presbyterian Historical Society, and the collection of Mr. Bruce Cotten.

The largest single collection of these North Carolina titles is in the Library of Congress, from which 81 titles are recorded. Next is the library of the University of North Carolina with 73 titles, followed by the Supreme Court Library, Raleigh, with 57, the Public Record Office, London, with 39, and the Harvard Law School Library, with 35. Other considerable collections are in the New York Public Library and in the Duke University Library, each having 29 titles, the Association of the Bar of New York City, 27 titles, the Historical Society of Pennsylvania, 21 titles, the Sondley Library at Asheville, 19 titles, and the American Antiquarian Society, 15 titles. Mr. Bruce Cotten has reported 29 titles from his collection.

Special mention must be made of the recent discovery of a veritable treasure-trove of eighteenth century North Carolina imprints in the Archives of the Moravian Church in America, Southern Province, located at Winston-Salem, North Carolina. These were reported in December, 1937, to the Historical Records Survey of the Works Progress Administration, in the course of its exploration of depositories of historical material. Immediate inquiry brought a report of 23 early North Carolina imprints in this Moravian library, with the altogether delightful surprise that six of them were previously unrecorded. These added five titles to our list of the journals of the colonial House of Assembly, as well as another issue of the laws of May, 1765, with the rare imprint of Andrew Steuart, and the printed proceedings of the Committee of Correspondence of Craven County, May, 1775. In addition to my acknowledgments of obligation to many librarians, as set forth below, I wish to express here my quite particular appreciation of the helpfulness of Miss Adelaide L. Fries in providing careful descriptions of the unique material found in the Moravian Archives.

With what subjects did these North Carolina books and pamphlets deal? A clear majority — 172 out of 288 — were official documents of one kind or another. But this proportion is nothing to wonder at, for the publications of government were the main dependence of most American colonial printers. The subjects are shown in the accompanying table.

Subject	Located	Not Located	Total
Almanacs	8	5	13
Court decisions:			
British	1		
North Carolina (state)	3	2	
United States	2		8
Funeral orations	5	1	6

Subject	Located	Not Located	Total
Military organizations and tactics	2	4	6
Political addresses	5	2	7
Revolutionary documents	7	4	11
"Regulators"	2		2
Religious sermons and tracts	18	10	
Baptist Ass'n minutes	8		36
Masonic proceedings and addresses	8	2	10
Domestic economy (farriery)	1		1
General literature	2	2	4
Law treatises and manuals	5	2	7
Medicine	1		1
School books		1	1
Science	1		1
Travel		1	1
North Carolina:			
Governor (messages and proclamations)			
Colonial	9	1	
State		1	11
Grand Jury:			
Colonial		1	
State		1	2
Legislature:			
Colonial:			
House journals	14	3	
address to governor	1		18
Council			
address to governor	1		1
State:			
General Assembly journals	2		
House journals	19		
Senate journals	15		36
Laws:			
Session:			
Colonial	21	1	
State	31		53
Collected:			
Colonial	5		
State	4		
Supplements to Iredell	11		20
Single:			
Colonial	1	2	
State	2	2	7
Provincial Congress	3		3
Tax schedules			
Colonial	1		
State	1		2
Comptroller	1		1

Subject	Located	Not Located	Total
Constitutional convention	5	1	6
University	1		1
United States:			
Articles of confederation	1		
Continental Congress	1		
Constitution (ratification)	1		
Laws		1	
Treatise		2	6
Not classified	6	2	8
Totals	237	53	290

Of the imprints recorded, 24 are broadsides. One specially interesting title, fully authenticated though not located, was printed in Gaelic (no. 164).

This bibliography has been in active preparation for over four years. During that period I have drawn heavily on friends and correspondents for information and aid. Without their generous cooperation it would have been impossible to bring the list to its present stage of completeness. My obligations are, therefore, numerous and extensive.

From two sources came important contributions to this bibliography. Miss Mary Thornton, in charge of the North Carolina collection of the University of North Carolina Library, generously placed at my disposal her own notes regarding North Carolina imprints not listed by Weeks, provided full descriptions of the imprints in the fine collection under her charge (an impressive number of which are not to be found elsewhere), and answered innumerable questions regarding bibliographical details. I wish to assure her of my gratitude for her competent and willing aid.

Professor Eldon R. James, librarian of the Harvard Law School, authorized me to have made, for the library under his able direction, complete photostats of all North Carolina session laws which were not represented by originals in that collection. These photostats, made from originals in the Public Record Office and in the University of North Carolina Library, passed through my hands and thus afforded me opportunity of writing descriptions of them at first hand. A reciprocal advantage is that the Harvard Law School now has available in original or photostat every North Carolina session law known to be extant, either at home or abroad. I am highly appreciative of this intelligent cooperation by Professor James.

To Mr. F. O. Poole, of the Association of the Bar of the City of of New York, and to Mr. John T. Vance, law librarian of the Library of Congress, I am indebted for answers to numerous inquiries regarding North Carolina legal imprints.

Mr. V. Valta Parma, curator of rare books at the Library of Congress, rendered highly appreciated aid toward the listing of legislative journals and other North Carolina imprints under his charge. Mr. L. Nelson Nichols, of the New York Public Library, courteously placed at my disposal the North Carolina titles in the notable imprints catalogue maintained by that institution and answered many questions regarding bibliographic minutiae. Mr. Willard O. Waters, of the Henry E. Huntington Library, furnished information regarding North Carolina titles in that great collection, for which I am grateful.

Mr. R. W. G. Vail, librarian of the American Antiquarian Society, rendered an uniquely valuable service to this bibliography by personally going through the files of North Carolina newspapers in the society's library and providing me with notes of contemporary advertisements of books and pamphlets published and offered for sale. And the compiler personally examined, for such advertisements, North Carolina newspaper files in several other important collections.

Mr. Bruce Cotten of Baltimore, whose private library contains a noteworthy collection of early North Carolina imprints, was unfailingly generous with information and provided descriptions of several titles, including one of which he appears to have the only known copy. Mr. Lawrence C. Wroth, librarian of the

John Carter Brown Library, contributed five otherwise unknown titles from the treasure house of colonial historical material over which he presides.

From librarians in North Carolina I received interested cooperation which resulted in bringing to light numerous titles heretofore unknown. I am particularly under obligation to Miss Philena A. Dickey, of the Sondley Reference Library, Asheville; to Miss Pierce, of the Charlotte Public Library; to Mrs. Ethel Taylor Crittenden, librarian at Wake Forest College; and to Professor J. P. Breedlove, the librarian of Duke University, as well as to Mr. E. Morrell and Miss Ruth A. Ketring, of the staff of that library.

Throughout the course of the work Mr. George A. Schwegmann, Jr., has kindly checked for me in the Union Catalog of the Library of Congress many North Carolina titles submitted to him. This appreciated service disclosed a considerable number of additional locations.

I am grateful to Mr. D. L. Corbitt, managing editor of the *North Carolina Historical Review,* in which much of the present material was published in 1936, for checking certain titles in the State Law Library.

Finally, I wish to express my sincere appreciation to my associate, Mr. Albert H. Allen, for his competent and painstaking assistance on the details of this bibliography and for the preparation of the accompanying statistical material and index.

It may be added that I shall appreciate note of any additional titles which may come to light or of additional locations of the imprints here recorded.

DOUGLAS C. MCMURTRIE

2039 North Magnolia Avenue
Chicago, Illinois
December 5, 1938.

KEY TO LOCATIONS

Note — As a rule, the first symbol is that of the library containing the copy from which the description was made. Then follow symbols for libraries in North Carolina, and then those for other libraries. Symbols for foreign libraries and private collections come last.

Andrews Mr. Alexander B. Andrews, Raleigh, N. C.
BrMus British Museum, London, England
CSmH Henry E. Huntington Library, San Marino, Cal.
Cotten Mr. Bruce Cotten, Baltimore
DLC Library of Congress, Washington
DSC Library of the Supreme Council, 33d Degree, Washington
ICJ John Crerar Library, Chicago
ICLaw Chicago Law Institute, Chicago
ICN Newberry Library, Chicago
ICU University of Chicago Library
IaCrM Iowa Masonic Library, Cedar Rapids
LHi Louisiana Historical Society, New Orleans.
M Massachusetts State Library, Boston
MB Boston Public Library
MBAt Library of the Boston Athenaeum
MBC Congregational Library, Boston
MH Harvard College Library, Cambridge
MH-L Harvard Law School Library, Cambridge
MHi Massachusetts Historical Society, Boston
MWA American Antiquarian Society, Worcester, Mass.
MiD-B Burton Historical Collection, Detroit Public Library

Mo	Missouri State Library, Jefferson City
MoS	Public Library, Saint Louis, Mo.
N	New York State Library, Albany, N. Y.
NHi	New York Historical Society, New York City
NIC	Cornell University Library, Ithaca, N. Y.
NN	New York Public Library
NNB	Association of the Bar, New York City
NNC	Columbia University, New York City
NNFM	Masonic Grand Lodge Library, New York City
NWM	United States Military Academy, West Point, N. Y.
Nc	North Carolina State Library, Raleigh
Nc-Law	Supreme Court Library, Raleigh, N. C.
NcAS	Sondley Library, Asheville, N. C.
NcC	Charlotte Public Library, Charlotte, N. C.
NcD	Duke University Library, Durham, N. C.
NcGW	Women's College of the University of North Carolina, Greensboro, N. C.
NcHiC	North Carolina Historical Commission, Raleigh
NcSaM	Archives of the Moravian Church, Southern Province, Winston-Salem, N. C.
NcU	University of North Carolina, Chapel Hill
NcW	Wilmington Public Library, Wilmington, N. C.
NcWfC	Wake Forest College, Wake Forest, N. C.
NjP	Princeton University, Princeton, N. J.
NjP-T	Princeton Theological Seminary, Princeton, N. J.
OC	Cincinnati Public Library, Cincinnati, Ohio
OCLaw	Cincinnati Law Library Association
PCA	American Baptist Historical Society, Chester, Pa.
PHi	Historical Society of Pennsylvania, Philadelphia
PPB	Bar Association Library, Philadelphia
PPFM	Masonic Grand Lodge Library, Philadelphia.
PPPrHi	Presbyterian Historical Society, Philadelphia
PRO	Public Record Office, London, England
PU-L	Biddle Law Library, University of Pennsylvania, Philadelphia
RPJCB	John Carter Brown Library, Providence, R. I.
RPL	Rhode Island Law Library, Providence
TKL	Lawson McGhee Library, Knoxville, Tenn.
WHi	Wisconsin Historical Society, Madison

BIBLIOGRAPHY

1749 — 1750

NORTH CAROLINA (*Colony*). *House of Burgesses.*
The | Journal | of the | House of Burgesses, | of the | Province of North-Carolina: | At a General Assembly, begun and held at Newbern, | the Twelfth Day of June, in the Nineteenth Year of the | Reign of our Sovereign Lord George the Second, by | the Grace of God, of Great-Britain, France, and Ireland, | King, Defender of the Faith, &c. and in the Year of our | Lord One Thousand Seven Hundred and Forty Six; and from | thence continued, by several Prorogations, to the Twenty | Sixth Day of September, in the Year of our Lord One Thou- | sand Seven Hundred and Forty Nine, in the Twenty Second | Year of His said Majesty's Reign: Being the Seventh Session | of this present General Assembly. | [*Rule*] | [2 *groups of ornaments*] | [*Rule*] | Newbern: | Printed and Sold by James Davis, M,DCC,XLIX.
18 x 31 cm. Title (verso blank), pp. 3-14. [1]
Contains the journal of the session from September 26 to October 18, 1749, with order of prorogation to "the Fourth Tuesday in March next; to be then held at Newbern."
"Monday, October 2, 1748 [i.e., 1749] .... Ordered, That the Clerk bring into this House the Revised Laws, which were laid before them the last

Session of Assembly, by the Commissioners appointed to Revise the same. And they were laid before the House accordingly." The House adjourned from day to day from October 2 until October 9, 1749, to permit an examination of the revised laws by the five members of the Council and a committee of eleven members of the House.

October 9, 1749, the revised laws were reported to the House for approval, and it was "Resolved, That the said Laws so Revised be Printed, by the Commissioners appointed for that Purpose."
PRO.

NORTH CAROLINA (*Colony*). *House of Burgesses.*
[2 *rules*] | The | Journal | of the | House of Burgesses. | [*Rule*] | [Newbern: James Davis, 1750.] [2]
19.5 x 30.5 cm. 4 p.
Caption title on p. 1; no imprint.
Covers the session from July 5 to July 10, 1750; at the last session the assembly was prorogued to the last Tuesday in September.
PRO.

1751 — 1752

NORTH CAROLINA (*Colony*). *House of Burgesses.*
[2 *rules*] | The | Journal | of the | House of Burgesses. | [*Rule*] | [Newbern: James Davis, 1751.] [3]
19 x 33 cm. pp. 3-20.
Caption title on p. 3; no imprint. Title page missing?
Covers the session from September 26 to October 12, 1751; prorogued to the second Tuesday in February, 1752.
PRO.

NORTH CAROLINA (*Colony*). *Laws, statutes, etc.*
Anno Regni | Georgii II, | Regis, Magnæ Brittanniæ, Franciæ, & | Hiberniæ, Vicessimo Quinto. | At a General Assembly begun and held at Newbern, the | Twelfth Day of June, in the Nineteenth Year of his | Majesty's Reign, and from thence continued, by Several | Prorogations, to the Twenty Seventh Day of September, | in the Year of our Lord One Thousand Seven Hundred | and Fifty One. | [Newbern: Printed by James Davis, 1751.]
19 x 28 cm. pp. 331-353. [4]

THE

JOURNAL

OF THE

HOUSE of BURGESSES,

OF THE

Province of *NORTH-CAROLINA*:

At a General ASSEMBLY, begun and held at *Newbern*, the Twelfth Day of *June*; in the Nineteenth Year of the Reign of our Sovereign Lord GEORGE the Second, by the Grace of God, of *Great-Britain, France*, and *Ireland*, King, Defender of the Faith, &c. and in the Year of our Lord One Thousand Seven Hundred and Forty Six; and from thence continued, by several Prorogations, to the Twenty Sixth Day of *September*, in the Year of our Lord One Thousand Seven Hundred and Forty Nine, in the Twenty Second Year of His said Majesty's Reign: Being the Seventh Session of this present General Assembly.

NEWBERN:
Printed and Sold by JAMES DAVIS, M,DCC,XLIX.

Caption title; no imprint. Has running head: Laws of North Carolina. Signatures P4 to U4; evidently a portion of the *Collection of all the Public Acts of Assembly*, Newbern, 1751, though possibly issued separately. CSmH. MH-L.

NORTH CAROLINA (*Colony*). *Laws, statutes, etc.*
A | Collection | of | All the Public | Acts of Assembly, | of | The Province of | North-Carolina: | Now in Force and Use. | Together with the Titles of all such Laws as are Obsolete, Ex- | pir'd, or Repeal'd. | And also, an exact Table of the Titles of the Acts in Force. | [*Rule*] | Revised by Commissioners appointed by an Act of the General As-|sembly of the said Province, for that Purpose; and Examined with the | Records, and Confirmed in full Assembly. | [*Rule*] | [*Group of ornaments*] | [*Rule*] | Newbern: Printed by James Davis, M,DCC,LI. [5]
19 x 28 cm. xii, [2], 353, [8] p.
Advertised in the *North-Carolina Gazette*, Newbern, November 15, 1751: "Lately published, and to be Sold by James Davis, at the Printing-Office in Newbern, The Whole Body of Laws of the Province of North Carolina: Revised by Commissioners appointed for that Purpose, Confirm'd in full Assembly. Published by Authority."
"The first issue of the North Carolina press that has survived to our day, and one of the first issued, was Swann's Revisal of the laws of the province." (Samuel B. Weeks, *The Press of North Carolina in the Eighteenth Century*, Brooklyn, 1891, p. 10.)
"Gov. Johnston, writing to the Board of Trade under date of Dec. 21, 1749, says the revised laws 'are now in the press and I expect to be able to send your Lordships a copy of them by the middle of June next' (*Col. Rec.*, IV, 924); but some new delay seems to have occurred. I have never heard of a Code printed in 1750." (Weeks, *op. cit.*, p. 13, footnote.)
A reissue of this volume was made in 1752, with the date on the title page changed and the laws of that year added. Dr. Wilberforce Eames wrote me in July, 1933: "I believe there were four issues of this book: — (1) with only the laws listed in the Table; (2) with the laws of 1751 added, not listed in the Table, NYPL; (3) with the laws of 1751 and 1752 added, not in the Table, HEH; and (4) like (3) but with 1752 title and a new Table." See no. 7.
Weeks no. 4.
NN. CSmH. NcAS. NcU. NcW. MH-L. NHi. PHi (Tower Coll).

A COLLECTION

OF

All the PUBLIC

ACTS OF ASSEMBLY,

OF

The PROVINCE of

NORTH-CAROLINA:

Now in FORCE and USE.

Together with the TITLES of all such LAWS as are Obsolete, Expir'd, or Repeal'd.

And also, an exact TABLE of the Titles of the ACTS in Force.

REVISED *by Commissioners appointed by an Act of the* GENERAL ASSEMBLY *of the said Province, for that Purpose; and Examined with the Records, and Confirmed in full Assembly.*

NEWBERN: Printed by JAMES DAVIS, M,DCC,LI.

North Carolina (*Colony*). *Laws, statutes, etc.*
Anno Regni | Georgii II, | Regis, Magnæ Brittanniæ, Franciæ, & | Hiberniæ, Vicessimo Quinto. | At a General Assembly, held at Bath-Town, the | Thirty First Day of March, in the Year of our Lord One | Thousand | Seven Hundred and Fifty Two. | [Newbern: Printed by James Davis, 1752.] [6]
19 x 28 cm. pp. 355-371.
Caption title; no imprint. Has running head: Laws of North Carolina. Evidently a portion of the *Collection of all the Public Acts of Assembly*, Newbern, 1752, though possibly issued separately and later included with the *Collection* of 1751 but with the new 1752 title page.
CSmH. MH-L. PHi.

North Carolina (*Colony*). *Laws, statutes, etc.*
A | Collection | of |All the Public | Acts of Assembly, | of | The Province of | North-Carolina. | Now in Force and Use. | Together with the Titles of all such Laws as are Obsolete, Ex- | pir'd, or Repeal'd. | And also, an exact Table of the Titles of the Acts in Force. | [*Rule*] | Revised by Commissioners appointed by an Act of the General As-|sembly of the said Province, for that Purpose; and Examined with the | Records, and Confirmed in full Assembly. | [*Rule*] | [*Group of ornaments*] | [*Rule*] | Newbern: Printed by James Davis, M,DCC,LII. [7]
19.5 x 28 cm. xii, 371, 2 p.
Title from reproduction of title page in *Acts and Laws of the Thirteen Original Colonies and State* (Russell Benedict Collection, American Art Association Auction Catalogue, February 27, 1922) No. 423, with collation as follows: Title, 1 leaf; Dedication, 1 leaf; Second Charter, xii p., Great Deed of Grant, 1 leaf; Acts, pp. 1-65, 67-77, 79-83, 85-101, 103-125, 127-173, 175-245, 247-291, 293-330, [331-334 missing], 335-353, and additional session law of 31 March, 1752) 355-371; Table, 2 p.
"These laws were printed in 1751, but the greater portion [in this edition] bear the date of 1752." Advertised in the *North-Carolina Gazette*, Newbern, March 6, 1752, as "Lately publish'd and to be sold by James Davis, at the Printing-Office in Newbern, . . ."
Weeks no. 5.
DLC. Nc. NcU. MH-L. MWA (imperfect) *N. NNB. NNC. PHi. Cotten.*

1753

[HALL, CLEMENT]
A | Collection | of many | Christian Experiences, Sentences, | and several | Places of Scripture Improved: | Also some short and plain Directions and Prayers | for sick Persons; with serious Advice to Persons | who have been Sick, to be by them perused and put | in Practice as soon as they are recovered; and a | Thanksgiving for Recovery. | To which is added, | Morning and Evening Prayers for Families and Chil-|dren, Directions for the Lord's Day, and some Cautions | against Indecencies in Time of Divine Service, &c. | Collected and Composed for the Spiritual Good of his Parish-|oners, and others. | By C. H. Missionary to the Honourable Society for the Propaga-|tion of the Gospel in Foreign Parts, and Rector of St. Paul's | Parish, in North Carolina. | [5 *lines*] | Newbern: | Printed by James Davis, M,DCC,LIII. [8]
51 p.

A second title page on p. 25 is as follows: Serious | Advice | to | Persons | Who have been Sick; To be by them perused and put in Practice as soon as | they are recovered: | With a Thanksgiving for Recovery. | Wrote by a Minister of the Church of England, for the | Spiritual Good of His Parishoners, &c. | [4 *lines*] | Newbern: | Printed by James Davis, M,DCC,-LIII.

No copy located. Title, as furnished by C. R. Hildeburn, from Stephen B. Weeks, *The Press of North Carolina in the Eighteenth Century* (Brooklyn, 1891), p. 55, no. 7.

NORTH CAROLINA (*Colony*). *House of Burgesses.*
The | Journal | of the | House of Burgesses, | of the | Province of North-Carolina: | At a General Assembly, begun and held at Newbern, | the Twelfth Day of June, in the Nineteenth Year of the | Reign of our Sovereign Lord George the Second, by | the Grace of God, of Great-Britain, France, and Ireland, | King, Defender of the Faith, &c. and in the Year of our | Lord One Thousand Seven Hundred and Forty Seven; and from | thence

[33]

continued, by several Prorogations, to the Thirty | First Day of March, in the Year of our Lord One Thou- | sand Seven Hundred and Fifty Two, in the Twenty Fifth Year of his said Majesty's Reign: Being the Eleventh Session of this | present General Assembly. | [2 *rules*] | [*Group of ornaments*] | [2 *rules*] | Newbern: Printed by James Davis, M,DCC,LIII. [9]
19.5 x 31 cm. 16 p.
Covers the session from March 31 to April 15, 1752; prorogued to "the second Tuesday in October next."
PRO.

North Carolina (*Colony*). *House of Burgesses.*
[2 *rules*] | The | Journal | of the | House of Burgesses. | [*Rule*] | [Newbern: James Davis, 1753.] [10]
19.5 x 32.5 cm. pp. 3-18.
Caption title on p. 3; no imprint. Title page missing?
Covers the session from March 28 to April 12, 1753; prorogued to the fourth Tuesday in September.
PRO.

North Carolina (*Colony*). *Laws, statutes, etc.*
[*Typographic headband*] | Anno Regni | Georgii II, | Regis Magnæ Brittanniæ, Franciæ, & | Hiberniæ, Vicessimo Sexto. | [*Rule*] | At a General Assembly, begun and held at New- | bern, the Twenty Seventh Day of March, in the Year of | our Lord One Thousand Seven Hundred and Fifty | Three. | [*Rule*] | [Newbern: Printed by James Davis, 1753.] [11]
19 x 30.5 cm. pp. 373-384.
Caption title; no imprint. Running head, between rules at top of page: Laws of North-Carolina. In margin, below the running head and above the headband: A. D. 1753. (Over a brace). Also in right margin, opposite the line "At a General Assembly, . . . ": Matthew | Rowan, Esq; | President. Pagination begins with p. 373 (signature C5), continuous with the *Collection of All the Public Acts*, edition of 1752.
Weeks no. 6 (not described nor located). Weeks 1896, no. *6a*, calls this a "Second edition," printed with changed page numbers "after the separate edition was struck off."
PRO. PHi.

[34]

THE JOURNAL

OF THE

HOUSE of BURGESSES,

OF THE

Province of *NORTH-CAROLINA*:

At a General ASSEMBLY, begun and held at *Newbern*, the Twelfth Day of *June*, in the Year of our Lord One Thousand Seven Hundred and Forty-seven, and in the Nineteenth Year of the Reign of our Sovereign Lord GEORGE the Second, by the Grace of God, of *Great-Britain, France,* and *Ireland,* King, Defender of the Faith, *&c.* and from thence continued, by several Prorogations and Adjournments, to the Third *Tuesday* in *February*, 1754; and then held at *Wilmington*: Being the Thirteenth Session of this present General Assembly.

NEWBERN:
Printed by JAMES DAVIS, M,DCC,LIV.

1754

North Carolina (*Colony*). *Governor (Arthur Dobbs)*.
A Message from His Excellency Arthur | Dobbs, Esq; Captain-General, and Go-|vernor in Chief, in and over his Majesty's | Province of North-Carolina; | To the General Assembly, held in Newbern, the Twelfth | Day of December, 1754. [12]
19.5 x 31.5 cm. 4 p.
Caption title; no imprint.
"Having in my Speech to you at your Meeting, told you that I should, in a most ample Manner, lay before you the Grand Plan of France, to ruin and distress all the English Colonies on this Continent; I take the earliest Opportunity of laying their wicked and enslaving Scheme before you, that you may see the Necessity there is of granting a reasonable and immediate Supply, and entering into a Plan of Union with all the British Colonies, for our mutual future Defence."
DLC.

North Carolina (*Colony*). *House of Burgesses*.
The | Journal | of the | House of Burgesses, | of the | Province of North-Carolina: | At a General Assembly, begun and held at Newbern, the Twelfth Day of June, in the Year of our Lord One | Thousand Seven Hundred and Forty-Seven, and in the Nine- | teenth Year of the Reign of our Sovereign Lord George | the Second, by the Grace of God, of Great-Britain, France, | and Ireland, King, Defender of the Faith, &c. and from | thence continued, by several Prorogations and Adjournments, | to the Third Tuesday in February, 1754; and then held at | Wilmington: Being the Thirteenth Session of this present | General Assembly. | [2 *rules*] | [*Group of ornaments*] | [2 *rules*] | Newbern: | Printed by James Davis, M,DCC,LIV. [13]
17 x 30.5 cm. 16 p.
PRO.

North Carolina (*Colony*). *Laws, statutes, etc.*
[*Typographic headband*] | Anno Regni | Georgii II, | Regis, Magnæ Britanniæ, Franciæ, & | Hiberniæ, Vicessimo Septimo.

[36]

| [*Rule*] | At a General Assembly, held at Wilmington, the | Nineteenth Day of February, in the Year of our Lord | One Thousand Seven Hundred and Fifty Four. | [*Rule*] | [Newbern: Printed by James Davis, 1754.] [14]
18.5 x 31 cm. pp. 385-410.
Caption title; no imprint. Running head, between rules at top of page: Laws of North-Carolina. In right margin, below the running head and above the headband: A. D. 1754. (Over a brace). Also in margin, opposite the line "At a General Assembly . . . "; Matthew | Rowan Esq; | President. Typographic elements in the headband different from those used in the preceding.
Pagination begins with p. 385 (signature F5).
Weeks no. 8.
PRO.

NORTH CAROLINA (*Colony*). *Laws, statutes, etc.*
A | Draught | of an | Act | Proposed to the Assembly | of | North-Carolina, | For Establishing a Paper Credit, | For 80,000 Pounds, Currency, | Upon a New Plan. | [*Row of typographic ornaments*] | Newbern: | Printed by James Davis, M,DCC,LIV. [15]
19 x 26 cm. 15 p.
Public Record Office copy has written on the title page: Recd. with Govr. Dobbs's Lettr. dated ye 4th Janry. 1775. Recd. July ye 2d. . . .
PRO.

[FRANKLIN, BENJAMIN]
[Franklin's Plan of Union. Newbern: Printed by James Davis, 1755.] [16]
Journal of the House of Burgesses, December 24, 1754: "Resolved that the consideration of the said plan be referred to the next session of Assembly and that in the meantime the printer print the same." (*Colonial Records of North Carolina*, vol. 5, p. 251.)
Weeks no. 9.

NORTH CAROLINA (*Colony*). *House of Burgesses.*
[2 *rules*] | The | Journal | of the | House of Burgesses. | [*Rule*] | [Newbern: Printed by James Davis, 1755 (?)] [17]
17.5 x 30 cm. 16 (?) p.

Caption title; no imprint. Title page missing in the copy described, which contains pp. 3 (with caption title) to 14; the text continues from p. 14. The last leaf is missing.

The Public Record Office copy would seem to have been received without the first leaf, containing the title page (if any). The clerical notation of receipt is written at the bottom of p. 3: Recd. with Govr. Dobbs's Lettr. dated ye 4th. Janry. 1755. Recd. July ye 2d. 1755.

The pages present cover the session from December 13 to December 23 (beginning on p. 14); the session lasted to January 15, 1755. Governor Dobbs apparently sent off only the pages that had been printed up to the date of his letter.

PRO.

NORTH CAROLINA (*Colony*). *Laws, statutes, etc.*
[*Typographic headband*] | Anno Regni | Georgii II, | Regis, Magnæ Britanniæ, Franciæ, & | Hiberniæ, Vicessimo Octavo. | [*Line of typographic ornaments*] | At a General Assembly, begun and held at Newbern, | on the Twelfth Day of December, in the Year of our Lord | One Thousand Seven Hundred and Fifty Four: Being the | first Session of this Assembly. | [*Line of other typographic ornaments*] | [Newbern: Printed by James Davis, 1755.] [18]

20 x 26.5 cm. pp. 3-63, [1] p. errata.

Caption title on p. 3 (Signature A); no imprint (title page missing ?). Running head, between rules at top of page: Laws of North-Carolina. In right margin, below the running head and above the headband: A. D. 1754. (Over a brace). Also in right margin, opposite the line "At a General Assembly . . .": Arthur | Dobbs, Esq; | Governor. Typographic elements in the headband slightly different from those in the preceding.

"Writing to the Board of Trade under date of Feb. 9, 1761, Gov. Dobbs says: 'I also sent to the Printer forthwith to furnish me with 4. setts of all the printed acts since my coming over, but as I believe several of them may now be out of print and will take up some time to reprint them I have charged him to lose no time in making up the setts for me, and that no money shall be paid him upon the printing until I have them from him, but as it is probable their Lordships may want a sett immediately I have sent about and have collected a complete sett, tho' much soiled.' " (Weeks, p. 56, from *Col. Rec.*, VI, 521.)

DRAUGHT

OF AN

ACT

Propoſed to the ASSEMBLY

OF

NORTH-CAROLINA,

For Eſtabliſhing a PAPER CREDIT,

For 80,000 Pounds, Currency,

Upon a NEW PLAN.

NEWBERN:
Printed by JAMES DAVIS, M,DCC,LIV.

In this copy the word "Vicessimo" appears to have been printed over the letters "Deci" or perhaps the word "Decimo."
Weeks no. 10 (not described nor located).
PRO.

NORTH CAROLINA (*Colony*). *Laws, statutes, etc.*
[*Typographic headband*] | Anno Regni | Georgii II, | Regis, Magnæ Britanniæ, Franciæ, & Hiberniæ, | Vicessimo Nono. | [*Rule*] | At a General Assembly, begun and held at Newbern, on | the Twelfth Day of December, in the Year of our Lord One | Thousand Seven Hundred and Fifty-four, and from thence | continued, by several Prorogations, to the Twenty-fifth Day | of September, in the Year of our Lord One Thousand Seven | Hundred and Fifty-five: Being the second Session of this | Assembly. | [*Rule*] | [Newbern: Printed by James Davis, 1755.]
20.5 x 32 cm. 30 p. [19]
Caption title on p. 1; no imprint. Running head between rules at top of page: Laws of North-Carolina. In right margin, below the running head and above the headband: A. D. 1755. (Over a brace). Also in right margin, as before, the name "Arthur Dobbs, Esq; Governor."
Typographic elements in headband the same as those used in the preceding, but in a slightly different arrangement. Page 1 has signature letter A.
Weeks no. 11 (not described nor located).
PRO.

1756

NORTH CAROLINA (*Colony*). *Laws, statutes, etc.*
[*Typographic headband*] | Anno Regni | Georgii II, | Regis, Magnæ Britanniæ, Franciæ, & Hiberniæ, | Tricessimo. | [*Rule*] | At a General Assembly, begun and held at Newbern, on | the Twelfth Day of December, in the Year of our Lord One | Thousand Seven Hundred and Fifty Four, and from thence | continued by several Prorogations, to the Thirtieth Day of | September, in the Year of our Lord One Thousand Seven | Hundred and Fifty Six; being the Third Session of this | Assembly. | [*Rule*] | [Newbern: Printed by James Davis, 1756.] [20]
20 x 32 cm. 38 p.

Caption title on p. 1; no imprint. Running head between rules at top of page: Laws of North-Carolina. In right margin, below the running head and above the headband: A. D. 1756. (Over a brace). Also in right margin, as before, the name "Arthur Dobbs, Esq; Governor."
Typographic elements in headband the same as those in the preceding, but reset with some of the elements wrongly placed. The words "Anno Regni" are here (and throughout the following including 1760) set in capitals. Page 1 has signature letter A.
Weeks no. 12 (not described nor located).
PRO.

SMITH, MICHAEL.
[A] | Sermon, | Preached in | Christ-Church, in Newbern, | in | North-Carolina | December the 27th, 1755, Aera of | Masonry, 5755, | Before | The Ancient and Honourable Society | of | Free and Accepted Masons. | [*Rule*] | Published at the Request of the Master, War-|dens, and Brethren of the Lodge. | [*Rule*] | By Michael Smith, A. B. | [*Rule*] | Newbern: | Printed by James Davis, M,DCC,LVI. [21]
9.5 x 15 cm. 19 p.
PHi (top of title page trimmed off).

1757

NORTH CAROLINA (*Colony*). *Governor* (*Arthur Dobbs*).
North-Carolina. | His Excellency Arthur Dobbs, Esq; Captain-General, Governor, and Commander in Chief, in and over the | Province of North-Carolina. | A Proclamation. | Whereas, The Honorable James Murray and John Rutherford, Esqrs. have issued a great Number of Notes | for Money,... | [9 *lines*] | Given under [my ha] nd, and the Great Seal of the said Province, at Newbern, the fifth Day of December, in the Thirty | First Year of his Maj [esty's] Reign, and in the Year of our Lord One Thousand Seven Hundred and Fifty Seven. | Arthur Dobbs. | By his Excellency's Command. | Richard Fenner, Dep. Sec. | God S [ave the] King. | [Newbern: James Davis, 1757.] [22]
31 x 19 cm. Broadside.

"... I have, by and with the Advice and Consent of his Majesty's Council, issued this my Proclamation, hereby forbidding the several Receivers of his Majesty's Quit-Rents, and the several Sherifs of the respective Counties in this Province, to receive the said Notes or Bills in Payment of any Arrears, Sum or Sums of Money, that now is, or hereafter may become due, for his Majesty's Quit-Rents, or any Public Taxes in this Province." See *Colonial Records,* V, 935-960, for an account of this case.
PRO.

North-Carolina. | I Promise that this Bill, for Twenty Shillings | Proclamation Money, shall be accepted from the Bearer, | by the Receiver-General, or his Deputy, in Payment of | Quit-rents and Arrears due to his Majesty, in the County of | New-Hanover, Bladen, Duplin, or Cumberland, for Va-|lue Received of [Messrs Gibson & Obryan] [1757.] [23]
12(?) x 6 cm.
In handwriting: Jany 24. 1757. To be pd. with Intt. from 10th April 1757 — Ja Murray J Rutherford
One of the "notes" referred to in Governor Dobbs's proclamation of December 5, 1757.
PRO.

NORTH CAROLINA (*Colony*). *Laws, statutes, etc.*
[*Typographic headband*] | Anno Regni | Georgii II, | Regis, Magnæ Britanniæ, Franciæ, & Hiberniæ, | Tricessimo. | [*Rule*] | At a General Assembly, begun and held at Newbern, on | the Twelfth Day of December, in the Year of our Lord One | Thousand Seven Hundred and Fifty-four, and from thence con- | tinued, by several Prorogations, to the Sixteenth Day of | May, in the Year of our Lord One Thousand Seven Hundred | and Fifty-seven: being the Fourth Session of this Assembly. | [*Rule*] | Newbern: Printed by James Davis, 1757.] [24]
18 x 30 cm. 5 p.
Caption title on p. 1; no imprint. Running head between rules at top of page: Laws of North-Carolina. In right margin, below the running head and above the headband: A. D. 1757. (Over a brace). But in this issue the printer omitted the name of Arthur Dobbs, Governor, in the right margin opposite the line "At a General Assembly ... "

SERMON,

PREACHED in
CHRIST-CHURCH, in NEWBERN,
IN
NORTH-CAROLINA,

December the 27th, 1755, Æra of
Masonry, 5755,

BEFORE

The Ancient and Honourable SOCIETY

OF

Free and Accepted MASONS.

Published at the Request of the Master, Wardens, and Brethren of the LODGE.

By MICHAEL SMITH, *A. B.*

NEWBERN:
Printed by JAMES DAVIS, M.DCC.LVI.

Typographic elements in the headband the same as on p. 385 of the laws of February 1754, but in 10 groups instead of 9 and with 4 of the main elements wrongly placed. Page 1 has signature letter A.
Weeks no. 13 (not described nor located).
PRO.

NORTH CAROLINA (*Colony*). *Laws, statutes, etc.*
[*Typographic headband*] | Anno Regni | Georgii II, | Regis, Magnæ Britanniæ, Franciæ, & Hiberniæ [*sic*], | Tricessimo Primo. | [*Rule*] | At a General Assembly, begun and held at Newbern, on the | Twelfth Day of December, in the Year of our Lord One Thousand Seven | Hundred and Fifty-four, and from thence continued, by several Prorogations, | to the Twenty-first Day of November, in the Year of our Lord One Thou-|sand Seven Hundred and Fifty-seven: being the Fifth Session of this As-|sembly. | [*Rule*] | [Newbern: Printed by James Davis, 1757.] [25]
18 x 31.5 cm. 15 p.
Caption title on p. 1; no imprint. Running head between rules at top of page: Laws of North-Carolina. In right margin, below the running head and above the headband: A. D. 1757. (Over a brace). Also in right margin, opposite the line "At a General Assembly . . .": Arth. Dobbs, Esq; Governor.
Typographic elements in headband mostly the same as those used in the laws of December 1754, but in a slightly different arrangement. Page 1 has signature letter A.
Weeks no. 14 (not described nor located).
PRO.

1758

NORTH CAROLINA (*Colony*). *Governor* (*Arthur Dobbs*).
North-Carolina. | By his Excellency Arthur Dobbs, Esq; Captain-General, and Governor | in Chief, in and over his Majesty's said Province. | A Proclamation. | [32 *lines*] | Given under my Hand and the Seal of the said Province, at Newbern, the Twenty-ninth Day of April, in | the Thirty-First Year of his Majesty's Reign, and in the Year of our Lord, One Thousand Seven Hun-

NORTH-CAROLINA:

By his Excellency *ARTHUR DOBBS*, Esq; Captain-General, and Governor in Chief, in and over his Majesty's said Province.

A PROCLAMATION.

WHEREAS the Enormity of our Sins, the Neglect of the Divine Service and Worship of God, and from our gross Sensualities and Immoralities, God Almighty has been pleased to correct *Britain* and these Colonies, by a heavy and dangerous War, by which we are in imminent Danger of losing the invaluable Blessing of our holy Religion, Liberties and Possessions: And whereas he has justly corrected these Colonies, by raising a Spirit in our *Indian* Neighbours, to invade, massacre, and make Prisoners, the *British* Inhabitants of these Colonies, upon their visible Neglect of the original native Inhabitants, by neither attempting to civilize, nor convert them to our holy Religion, and therefore God Almighty has left us, more immediately to be punished by them, at the Instigation of our cruel and inveterate Enemies the *French*, who, from their Principles, endeavour to extirpate the Protestant Religion wherever they have Power; and have not only in these Provinces, but in *Europe*, formed a formidable *Popish* League, to extirpate and ruin the Protestant Interest of *Europe*: And whereas it appears, that after a short Correction of the Protestants in *Germany*, God Almighty has most wonderfully manifested himself in Defence of the Protestant Cause in *Germany*, and has apparently headed their Armies, by inspiring them with an invincible Courage, and conducting their Councils, and at the same Time dispiriting their *Popish* Enemies, and turning all their Councils into Foolishness, so that it manifestly appears that God will not desert the holy Protestant Religion, provided we, with humble Hearts, sincerely repent of our gross Sensualities and Immoralities, and our shameful Neglect of his Divine Service and Worship, and serve him and his Christ with our whole Hearts, and not with only a Lip-Service, and external Worship.

Let us therefore, with sincere Hearts, fall down before him, and supplicate him, through the Merits and Satisfaction of his dear Son Christ Jesus, our only Mediator and Redeemer, to forgive us our Sins, upon our sincere Resolution of Amendment; and that he will avert those Judgments hanging over us, accept of the Punishments already poured out upon us, and leave us no longer to be corrected by our Enemies, but that he will restore us to his Favour, go out and lead our Armies, Fleets and Councils, and inspire us with Courage to defend our holy Religion, and Civil Liberties; and to return him the utmost Praise for manifesting himself so eminently in Defence of the Protestant Interest, and Civil Liberties of *Europe*, with a lively Hope and Faith, that if we repent and amend, that he will also manifest himself as the God and Protector of the Protestant Cause, and Liberties of *Britain* and these Colonies, and implore a Blessing on his Majesty's Arms and Councils.

As therefore a Day of public Fasting and Humiliation is, at this critical Time, most highly necessary, I have, by the Advice of his Majesty's honourable Council, thought fit to issue this my Proclamation, and do hereby appoint *Wednesday* the Seventh of *June* next, to be kept holy by all Ranks of People within this Province, as a Day of Fasting and Supplication; and also to give Thanks to Almighty God, and our blessed Saviour Christ Jesus, for having hitherto preserved this Province in Peace, in the Midst of surrounding impending Dangers, and on Account of the Manifestation of his Providence, so remarkable in protecting the Protestant Interest, and Civil Liberties of *Europe*, from the united *Popish* Powers, hoping also that he will declare himself the Protector of the Protestant Interest in *America*, lead our Armies and Councils, and give a Blessing to the Arms of his most gracious Majesty by Sea and Land; and that he may support our religious and civil Liberties, and may vanquish and overcome our insatiable and inveterate Enemies.

I therefore strictly command and require, that Public Service be had in all Churches and Chappels within this Province, and that it be kept holy, from all manual Labour, and that this Proclamation be publickly read, either on that Day, or some convenient *Sunday* before it, to give Notice to all Persons within this Province, to pay a Regard and Obedience to it.

GIVEN *under my Hand and the Seal of the said Province, at Newbern, the Twenty-ninth Day of April, in the Thirty-First Year of his Majesty's Reign, and in the Year of our Lord, One Thousand Seven Hundred and Fifty-eight.*

By his Excellency's Command,
Richard Fenner, Dep. Sec.

ARTHUR DOBBS.

GOD Save the KING.

dred and | Fifty-eight. | By his Excellency's Command, | Richard Fenner, Dep. Sec. | Arthur Dobbs. | God Save the King. [26]
31.5 x 30.5 cm. Broadside.
Appoints "Wednesday the Seventh of June next" as a day of public fasting and humiliation, in view of the pending war with France.
PRO.

NORTH CAROLINA (*Colony*). *Laws, statutes, etc.*
[*Typographic headband*] | Anno Regni | Georgii II, | Regis, Magnæ Britanniæ, Franciæ, & Hiberniæ, | Tricessimo Primo. | [*Rule*] | At a General Assembly, begun and held at Newbern, | on the Twelfth Day of December, in the Year of our Lord One | Thousand Seven Hundred and Fifty-four, and from thence con- | tinued, by several Prorogations, to the Twenty-eighth Day of | April, in the Year of our Lord, One Thousand Seven Hun- | dred and Fifty-eight; being the Sixth Session of this Assembly. | [*Rule*] | [Newbern: Printed by James Davis, 1758.] [27]
18 x 31 cm. 8 p.
Caption title on p. 1; no imprint. Running head between rules at top of page: Laws of North-Carolina. In right margin, below running head and above headband: A. D. 1758. (Over a brace). Also in right margin, as in preceding: Arth. Dobbs, | Esq; Governor.
Headband made up of only one typographic element; one piece wrongly placed. Page 1 has signature letter A.
Weeks no. 15 (not described nor located).
PRO.

NORTH CAROLINA (*Colony*). *Laws, statutes, etc.*
[*Typographic headband*] | Anno Regni | Georgii II, | Regis, Magnæ, [*sic*] Britanniæ, Franciæ, & Hiberniæ, | Tricessimo Secundo. | [*Rule*] | At a General Assembly, begun and held at New-|bern, on the Twelfth Day of December, in the Year of our | Lord One Thousand Seven Hundred and Fifty-four, and from | thence continued, by several Prorogations, to the Twenty-third | Day of November, in the Year of our Lord One Thousand | Seven Hundred and Fifty-eight, then held at Edenton; being |

the Seventh Session of this Assembly. | [*Rule*] | [Newbern: Printed by James Davis, 1758.] [28]
18.5 x 32.5 cm. 31 p.
Caption title on p. 1; no imprint. Running head between rules at top of page: Laws of North-Carolina. In right margin, below running head and above headband: A. D. 1758. (Over a brace). Also in right margin, as in preceding, the name Arth. Dobbs, Esq; Governor.
Headband almost wholly as in the preceding, but with a slight difference in the arrangement. Page 1 has signature letter A.
Weeks no. 16 (not described nor located).
PRO.

STEWART, ALEXANDER.
The | Validity | of | Infant | Baptism. | [*Rule*] | By A. Stewart, A. M. Minister of | Beaufort County, North-Carolina. | [*Rule*] | [*Double rule*] | Newbern: | Printed by James Davis. | [*Short rule*] | M,DCC,LVIII. [29]
9.5 x 16 cm. 40 p.
"In 1759, Rev. Alexander Stewart, then pastor of St. Thomas' Parish, Bath, compiled 'a small tract collected from the best authors I could here find' in defense of baptism as practiced by the Established Church. This was printed and 400 copies were distributed through the province. It was aimed at the Baptists, who were then growing, and 'for some time checked their proceedings.'" (*Colonial Records,* VI, 316, cited by Weeks 1896, p. 252.)
Sabin 91624.
MH.

1759 — 1760

NORTH CAROLINA (*Colony*). *Laws, statutes, etc.*
[*Typographic headband*] | Anno Regni | Georgii II, | Regis, Magnæ, [*sic*] Britanniæ, Franciæ, & Hiberniæ, | Tricessimo Tertio. | [*Rule*] | At a General Assembly, begun and held at New-|bern, on the Twelfth Day of December, in the Year of our | Lord One thousand Seven Hundred and Fifty-four, and from | thence continued, by several Prorogations, to the Eighth Day | of May, in the Year of our Lord One Thousand Seven

Hun-|dred and Fifty-nine, to be then held at Newbern; being the | Eighth Session of Assemby [*sic*]. | [*Rule*] | [Newbern: Printed by James Davis, 1759.] [30]
19 x 31.5 cm. 3 p.
Caption title on p. 1; no imprint. Running head between rules at top of page: Laws of North-Carolina. In right margin, below running head and above headband: A. D. 1759. (Over a brace). Also in right margin, as before, the name Arth. Dobbs, Esq; Governor.
The main typographic element in the headband is that used on p. 373, laws of March 1753, but in a somewhat different arrangement. No signature letter appears on p. 1.
Weeks no. 17 (not described nor located).
PRO.

NORTH CAROLINA (*Colony*). *Laws, statutes, etc.*
[*Typographic headband*] | Anno Regni | Georgii II, | Regis Magnæ, [*sic*] Britanniæ, Franciæ, & Hiberniæ, | Tricessimo Tertio. | [*Rule*] | At a General Assembly, begun and held at New-|bern, on the Twelfth Day of December, in the Year of our | Lord One Thousand Seven Hundred and Fifty-four, and from | thence continued, by several Prorogations, to the Twentieth | Day of November, in the Year of our Lord One Thousand Se-|ven Hundred and Fifty-nine, then held at Wilmington; being | the Ninth Session of this Assemby [*sic*]. | [*Rule*] | [Newbern: Printed by James Davis, 1760.] [31]
18.5 x 27 cm. 19 p.
Caption title on p. 1; no imprint. Running head between rules at top of page: Laws of North-Carolina. In right margin, below running head and above headband: A. D. 1759. (Over a brace). Also in right margin, as before, the name Arth. Dobbs, Esq; Governor.
Headband the same as in the preceding. Page 1 has signature letter A.
Weeks no. 18 (not described nor located).
PRO.

NORTH CAROLINA (*Colony*). *Laws, statutes, etc.*
[*Typographic headband*] | Anno Regni | Georgii II, | Regis, Magniæ, [*sic*] Britanniæ, Franciæ, & Hiberniæ, | Tricessimo

THE
VALIDITY
OF
INFANT
BAPTISM.

By *A. STEWART*, A. M. Minister of *Beaufort* County, NORTH-CAROLINA.

NEWBERN:
Printed by JAMES DAVIS.
M,DCC,LVIII.

Tertio. | [*Rule*] | At an Assembly, begun and held at Newbern, the Twen-|ty-fourth Day of April, in the Thirty-third Year of the Reign | of our Sovereign Lord George the Second, by the | Grace of God, of Great-Britain, France, and Ireland, | King, &c. and in the Year of our Lord One Thousand Seven | Hundred and Sixty; being the First Session of this presen | Assembly. | [*Rule*] | [Newbern: Printed by James Davis, 1760.]   [32]
19 x 26 cm. 32 p.

Caption title on p. 1; no imprint. Running head between rules at top of page: Laws of North-Carolina. In right margin below running head and above headband: A. D. 1760. (Over a brace). Also in right margin, as before, the name Arth. Dobbs, Esq; Governor.

Headband the same as in the laws of April 1758, but correctly composed. Page 1 has signature letter A.

Weeks no. 19 (not described nor located).
PRO.

NORTH CAROLINA (*Colony*). *Laws, statutes, etc.*
[*Typographic headband*] Anno Regni | Georgii II, | Regis, Magniæ, [*sic*] Britanniæ, Franciæ, & Hiberniæ, Tricessimo Tertio. | [*Rule*] | At an Assembly, begun and held at Newbern, the Twen-|ty-fourth Day of April, in the Thirty-third Year of the Reign | of our Sovereign Lord George the Second, by the | Grace of God, of Great-Britain, France, and Ireland, | King, &c. and from thence continued, by Prorogation, to | the Twenty-sixth Day of May, in the Year of our Lord One | Thousand Seven Hundred and Sixty; being the Second Ses-|sion of this present Assembly. | [*Rule*] | [Newbern: Printed by James Davis, 1760.]
18.5 x 30 cm. (trimmed close at top). 14 p.   [33]

Caption title on p. 1; no imprint. Running head between rules at top of page: Laws of North-Carolina. In right margin below running head and above headband: A. D. 1760. (Over a brace). Also in right margin, as before, the name Arth. Dobbs, Esq; Governor.

Headband the same as in the preceding. Page 1 has signature letter A.
Weeks no. 20 (not described nor located).
PRO.

NORTH CAROLINA (*Colony*). *Laws, statutes, etc.*
[*Typographic headband*] Anno Regni | Georgii II, | Regis, Magniæ, [*sic*] Britanniæ, Franciæ, & Hiberniæ, Tricessimo Quarto. | [*Rule*] | At an Assembly, begun and held at Newbern, the Twen-|ty-fourth Day of April, in the Thirty-third Year of the Reign | of our Sovereign Lord George the Second, by the | Grace of God, of Great-Britain, France, and Ireland, | King, &c. and from thence continued, by several Proroga-|tions, to the Twenty-sixth Day of June, in the Year of our | Lord One Thousand Seven Hundred and Sixty; to be then | held at Wilmington; Being the Third Session of this present | Assembly. | [*Rule*] | [Newbern: Printed by James Davis, 1760.] [34]
17.5 x 31.5 cm. 7 p.
Caption title on p. 1; no imprint. Running head between rules at top of page: Laws of North-Carolina. In right margin below running head and above headband: A. D. 1760. (Over a brace). Also in right margin, as before, the name of Arth. Dobbs, Esq; Governor.
Headband the same as in the two preceding. Page 1 has signature letter A. Weeks no. 21 (not described nor located).
PRO.

1761

CAMP,
[Sermon preached before the General Assembly on April 12, 1761, by the Rev. Mr. Camp. Newbern: Printed by James Davis, 1761.] [35]
Title from Weeks, no. 23, who cites *Colonial Records,* VI, 684, 688, and 823. On Monday, April 13, 1761, the lower house of the assembly "Ordered Mr. Sampson and Mr. Harnett, wait on the Reverend Mr. Camp, and return him the thanks of this House, for his Sermon Preached before them Yesterday, and request a Copy thereof, that this House may direct the same to be printed." On April 24, 1762, Davis petitioned the house that he be allowed pay "for printing and dispersing four Hundred Copies of the Reverend Mr. Camp's Sermons, which he has done by order of the Assembly." The petition was referred to the Committee of Claims, and existing records do not disclose what became of it.

NORTH CAROLINA (*Colony*). *Laws, statutes, etc.*
[Acts passed by the General Assembly during the session of November and December, 1760. Newbern: James Davis, 1761.]
[36]
Weeks no. 22. These session laws were undoubtedly printed, though no copy can now be found. There are no laws for this session in the set sent to the Board of Trade by Governor Dobbs in February, 1761, referred to in the note to Weeks no. 10. The session of June, 1760, is the last represented in this set, now in the Public Record Office.

1762

NICHOLSON, THOMAS.
[2 *rules*] | An Epistle | to | Friends in Great Britain, | To whom is the Salutation of my Love, in the | unchangeable Truth. | [Newbern: James Davis ? 1762.] [37]
13 x 20 cm. 4 p.
Caption title; no imprint. Signed and dated at end: Thomas Nicholson. | Little River in North | Carolina, the 15th | of the Ninth Month | 1762.
Sabin 55234.
N. NN. BrMus.

NORTH CAROLINA (*Colony*). *House of Assembly.*
[*Row of type ornaments*] | The | Journal | of the | House of Assembly. | [*Row of type ornaments*] | North-Carolina, ss. | At an Assembly, begun and held at Wilmington, the Thirteenth Day of April, One Thousand Seven Hundred and | Sixty-two; and in the Second Year of the Reign of our So-|vereign Lord George the Third, by the Grace of God, | of Great-Britain, France, and Ireland, King, Defender of the | Faith, &c. Being the First Meeting of this present Assembly. | [*Rule*] | [Newbern: James Davis, 1762.] [38]
19 x 26 cm. 28 p.
Caption title; no imprint.
See *Colonial Records*, VI, 965, 967, Governor Dobbs to Lord Egremont, February 23, 1763, and to the Board of Trade, same date, referring to the "printed Journal herewith sent" in duplication of copies sent "the 30th of April last."

This Assembly resisted efforts of the governor to procure grants of funds and troops as required by the British authorities in England. Prorogued April 19th to meet in second session on April 20; prorogued April 23 to meet in third session April 24th. On April 29 Governor Dobbs dismissed the Assembly with a sharp message.
PRO.

NORTH CAROLINA (*Colony*). *House of Assembly.*
[The Journal of the House of Assembly. North Carolina. At an Assembly, begun and held at Wilmington, the third day of November, One Thousand Seven Hundred and Sixty-two; and in the Second Year of the Reign of our Sovereign Lord George the Third, by the Grace of God, of Great Britain, France, and Ireland, King, Defender of the Faith, &c. Being the Second Meeting of the present Assembly. Newbern: James Davis, 1762.]
[39]
Title, following the form of the title of the house journal of the session of April, 1762, based on Weeks no. 24, who cites *Colonial Records*, VI, 962. On December 11, 1762 the house "Resolved that James Davis Printer do print the Laws passed this Session and the Journals of this Assembly, . . . and that he be paid by the public Treasurer for the same the sum of Two Hundred pounds proc Money, . . . " On receiving this resolution, the council replied ". . . . . We think the Sum much too great for the service he is to perform and cannot agree thereto, . . . " and proposed "to continue the Act Appointing him Printer for six Months longer." In this the house would not concur, and before the matter could be settled the governor prorogued the assembly.

NORTH CAROLINA (*Colony*). *Laws, statutes, etc.*
[*Headband of type ornaments*] | Anno Regni | Georgii III, | Regis, Magnæ Britanniæ, Franciæ, & Hiberniæ, | Tertio. | [*Rule*] | At an Assembly, begun and held at Newbern, the Third | Day of November, in the Third Year of the Reign of our Sove- | reign Lord George the Third, by the Grace of God, of | Great- Britain, France, and Ireland, King, &c. and in the Year | of our Lord One Thousand Seven Hundred and Sixty-two, be- | ing the

First Session of this present Assembly. | [*Rule*] | [Newbern: Printed by James Davis, 1762.] [40]
19.5 x 26 cm. 28+ p.
Caption title on p. 1; no imprint. Running head between rules at top of page: Laws of North-Carolina. In right margin below running head and above headband: A. D. 1762 (over a brace). Also in right margin, opposite the line "At an Assembly . . .": Arth. Dobbs, | Esq; Governor.
See *Colonial Records,* VI, 962, quoted in note on the preceding title.
Weeks no. 24 (not located).
NcU (lacking all after p. 28).

1763

NORTH CAROLINA (*Colony*). *Laws, statutes, etc.*
[An Act for the More Effectual Observing of the Queen's Peace and Establishing a Good and Lasting Foundation of Government in North Carolina. Newbern: Printed by James Davis, 1763.] [41]
Ordered to be printed by the Governor and Council April 22, 1763, according to *Colonial Records,* VI, 1013, cited by Weeks, no. 26. The printer was to "Print as many Copys of the said Act as he has printed or shall print of the Laws passed last session of Assembly, and he shall Transmit a Copy of the said Act with each Copy of the said late Laws, for which service he shall be allowed a Claim on the Publick."

REID, JAMES.
[Sermon Recommending the Establishing Public Schools for the Education of Youth, preached before the General Assembly in November, 1762, by Rev. James Reid. Newbern: Printed by James Davis, 1763.] [42]
Mr. Reid was "desired to furnish the Printer with a copy thereof, in order that the same may be printed and dispersed in the several counties within this Province" according to *Colonial Records,* VI, 955.

1764

NORTH CAROLINA (*Colony*). *House of Assembly.*
[The Journal of the House of Assembly. North Carolina, ss. At an Assembly, begun and held at Wilmington, the thirtieth day of

January, One Thousand Seven Hundred and Sixty-four; and in the Fourth Year of the Reign of our Sovereign Lord George the Third, by the Grace of God, of Great Britain, France, and Ireland, King, Defender of the Faith, &c. Being the Second Meeting of the present Assembly. Newbern: James Davis, 1764.] [43]
Title, in the form of titles of earlier house journals, based on Weeks nos. 27 and 28, who cites *Colonial Records,* VII, 334.

NORTH CAROLINA (*Colony*). *Laws, statutes, etc.*
Anno Regni | Georgii III. Regis | Magnæ Britanniæ, Franciæ, & Hiberniæ, | Quinto. | At an Assembly begun and held at Wilmington, the Third Day of | February, in the Fourth Year of the Reign of our Sovereign Lord George | the Third, by the Grace of God, of Great-Britain, France and Ireland, | King, Defender of the Faith, &c. and in the Year of our Lord, One Thousand, | Seven Hundred and Sixty-four; and from thence continued, by Prorogations, to | the Twenty-fifth Day of October, in the Fifth Year of the Reign of our said | Sovereign Lord George the Third, &c. and in the Year of our Lord One | Thousand, Seven Hundred and Sixty-four, to be then held at Wilmington, | Being the Second Session of this present Assembly; | The following Laws were Enacted. | [*2 rules*] | [*Royal arms*] | [*3 rules*] | Wilmington: | Printed by Andrew Steuart, (by Virtue of His Majesty's Royal Com-|mission to him granted, bearing Date November 27, 1764.) [44]
19 x 32 cm. [2], 28 p.
The first printing done by Steuart during his brief tenure of office, under appointment by Governor Dobbs, as "King's Printer" in North Carolina. The assembly appointed James Davis printer and forbade the payment of any money to Steuart beyond 100 pounds in North Carolina currency to reimburse him for his trouble in coming to the province.
Weeks no. 27 (not located).
NcU (lacks all after p. 22).

NORTH CAROLINA (*Colony*). *Laws, statutes, etc.*
A | Collection | of all the | Acts of Assembly, | of | The Province

[55]

of | North-Carolina, | In Force and Use, | Since the Revisal of the Laws of the Year 1751. | Together with the Titles of all such Laws as are | Obsolete, had their Effect, Expir'd or Repealed. | With an exact Table. | To which is prefixed, | A List of the Names of those Gentlemen who subscribed | for the Book. | [*Rule*] | [*2 groups of type ornaments*] | [*Rule*] | Newbern: | Printed by James Davis, M,DCC,LXIV. [45]
18 x 24.5 cm. [1], 386, [4] p.
Contains (p. 309-386) the laws of the sessions of 1764, which do not appear to have been printed separately except for the laws of the session of October-November, 1764, which were printed by Andrew Steuart (no. 44, above.)
This collection was the work of James Davis and is commonly referred to as Davis's First Revisal.
Weeks no. 29 (collated but not located). Sabin 55601.
NN. Nc-Law. NcU. NHi (lacks portion of p. 385-6). *NNB.*

1765

MOORE, MAURICE.
Justi[ce and Policy] | of Taxing | The American Colonies, | In Great-Britain, considered: | Wherein is shewed, | That the Colonists are not a conquered People:—That | they are constitutionally intituled to be taxed only by their | own Consent:—And that the imposing a Stamp-Duty | on the Colonists is as impolitic as it is inconsistant with | their Rights. | Non sibi sed patriæ. | By Maurice Moore, Esquire. | Wilmington, [North-Carolina] | Printed by Andrew Steuart, and sold at his Office, near | the Exchange. M,DCC,LXV. [46]
10 x 16.5 cm. 16 p.
Reprinted in *North Carolina University Magazine*, v. 1, 1852, p. 71-77 and 85-87. And see William K. Boyd, *Some Eighteenth Century Tracts Concerning North Carolina* (Raleigh, 1927), p. 159-174 (with reproduction of the title page on p. 163.)
Weeks no. 32 (not located) mentions the reprint of 1852 and says that a copy of the original "was in possession of the N. C. Historical Society at the time of republication, but . . . has since disappeared." Evans 10076.
NcU (upper part of title page torn off). *RPJCB. ICN* has photostatic copy.

Anno Regni

GEORGII III. REGIS

MAGNÆ BRITANNIÆ, FRANCIÆ, & HIBERNIÆ,

QUINTO.

AT AN ASSEMBLY begun and held at WILMINGTON, the Third Day of FEBRUARY, in the Fourth Year of the Reign of our Sovereign Lord GEORGE the THIRD, by the Grace of GOD, of GREAT-BRITAIN, FRANCE and IRELAND, King, Defender of the Faith, &c. and in the Year of our Lord, One Thoufand, Seven Hundred and Sixty-four; and from thence continued, by Prorogations, to the Twenty-fifth Day of OCTOBER, in the Fifth Year of the Reign of our faid Sovereign Lord GEORGE the THIRD, &c. and in the Year of our Lord, One Thoufand, Seven Hundred and Sixty-four, to be then held at WILMINGTON, Being the SECOND SESSION of this prefent ASSEMBLY;

The following LAWS were ENACTED.

WILMINGTON:

Printed by ANDREW STEUART, (by Virtue of His MAJESTY's Royal Com- miffion to him granted, bearing Date November 27, 1764.)

NORTH CAROLINA (*Colony*). *House of Assembly.*
[The Journal of the House of Assembly. North Carolina. At an Assembly, begun and held at Wilmington, the third day of February, in the fourth year of the Reign of our Sovereign Lord George the Third, by the Grace of God, of Great-Britain, France, and Ireland, King, Defender of the Faith, &c. and in the Year of our Lord One Thousand Seven Hundred and Sixty-Four; and from thence continued, by several Prorogations, to the Third Day of May, in the Fifth Year of the Reign of our said Sovereign Lord George the Third, &c. and in the Year of our Lord One Thousand Seven Hundred and Sixty-Five; to be then held at Newbern; being the Third Session of this present Assembly. Newbern: Printed by James Davis, 1765.] [47]
Title, in the form of titles of earlier house journals, based on Weeks no. 30, who cites *Colonial Records,* VII, 59, 64, 86.

On March 16, 1765, the house adopted a resolution that ten pounds be paid to William Godfrey for "Transmitting a copy of the Laws of last session of Assembly from Wilmington to James Davis, Printer in Newbern." (*Colonial Records,* VII, 58, 85.)

On May 6, 1765, "Mr. Montfort moved that the Clerk furnish James Davis, Printer, with a Copy of the Journal of the House daily, and that he acquaint the said James Davis the House direct him to print the same & dispense the Copys so printed to each Member of the House." (*Colonial Records,* VII, 64.)

NORTH CAROLINA (*Colony*). *Laws, statutes, etc.*
[*Headband of type ornaments*] | Anno Regni | Georgii III, | Regis, Magnæ Britanniæ, Franciæ, & Hiberniæ, | Quinto. | [*Rule*] | At an Assembly begun and held at Wilmington, | the Third Day of February, in the Fourth Year of the | Reign of our Sovereign Lord George the Third, by the | Grace of God, of Great-Britain, France, and Ireland, | King, Defender of the Faith, &c. and in the Year of our | Lord One Thousand Seven Hundred and Sixty-four; and | from thence continued, by several Prorogations, to the Third | Day of May, in the Fifth Year of the Reign of our said | Sovereign Lord George the Third, &c.

and in the | Year of our Lord One Thousand Seven Hundred and Sixty- | five; to be then held at Newbern: Being the Third Session of this present Assembly. | [*Rule*] | [Newbern: Printed by James Davis, 1765.] [48]
19.5 x 26.5 cm. Pages 387-393. Signatures D5-E5, each 2 leaves.
Caption title on p. 387; no imprint. Running head between rules at top of page: Laws of North-Carolina. In right margin, below running head and above headband: A. D. 1765 (over a brace). Also in right margin, opposite the line "At an Assembly . . . ": Wil. Tryon, | Esq; Lieutenant | Governor.
At end, p. 393: "Read Three Times, and Ratified in open Assembly, the 18th Day of May, A. D. 1765."
A printed copy of the laws of May 18, 1765, in the Fulham Palace Library, London, is noted by Charles M. Andrews and Frances E. Davenport, *Guide to the Manuscript Materials for the History of the United States to 1783, in . . . London Archives . . .* (Washington, 1908), p. 321.
Weeks no. 30 (not located). Evans 10107 (from Weeks).
NcU.

NORTH CAROLINA (*Colony*). *Laws, statutes, etc.*
Anno Regni | Georgii III. Regis | Magnae Britanniæ, Francæ [*sic*], & Hiberniæ, | Quinto. | At an Assembly begun and held at Wilmington, the Third Day | of February, in the Fourth Year of the Reign of our Sovereign Lord George | the Third, by the Grace of God, of Great Britain, France and Ireland, King, | Defender of the Faith, &c. and in the Year of our Lord, One Thousand, Seven | Hundred and Sixty-four, and from thence continued, by Prorogations, to the | Third Day of May, in the Fifth Year of the Reign of our said Sovereign Lord | George the Third, &c. and in the Year of our Lord, One Thousand | Seven Hundred and Sixty-five, and then held at Newbern; being the | Third Session of this present Assembly. | The following Laws were enacted. | [*Double rule*] | [*Royal arms*] | [*Double rule*] | Wilmington: | Printed by Andrew Steuart, Printer to the King's most excellent | Majesty. M,DCC,LXV. [49]
19 x 32 cm. p. 29-32.

Evidently paged continuously with Steuart's printing of the laws of the session of October, 1764; see no. 44, above.
NcSaM. NHi.

NORTH CAROLINA (*Colony*). *Laws, statutes, etc.*
A | Collection | of All the | Acts of Assembly, | of the Province of | North Carolina, | Now in Force and Use. Together | with the Titles of all such Laws as are | Obsolete, Expired or Repealed. | In two Volumes. | With | Marginal Notes and References, and an exact Table | to the Whole. | [*Rule*] | Volume I. | [*Rule*] | Printed by James Davis, Printer to the Honourable the Commons | House of Assembly. M DCC LXV.   [50]
19.5 x 24 cm. Two vols. in one. Vol. I, xvi, 176 p.; Vol. II, 393 p. and [21] p. index.
Weeks no. 31.
NNB. Nc-Law. NcU. NN. BrMus.

1766

NORTH CAROLINA (*Colony*). *Laws, statutes, etc.*
[*Headband of type ornaments*] | Anno Regni | Georgii III, | Regis, | Magnæ Britanniæ, Franciæ, & Hiberniæ, | Septimo. | [*Rule*] | At an Assembly begun and held at Newbern, the | Third Day of November, in the Seventh Year of the Reign | of our Sovereign Lord George the Third, by the | Grace of God, of Great-Britain, France, and Ireland, | King, Defender of the Faith, &c. and in the Year of our | Lord, One Thousand Seven Hundred and Sixty Six: Being | the First Session of this present Assembly. | [*Rule*] | [Newbern: James Davis, 1766.]   [51]
21.5 x 28 cm. p. 395-438. Signatures F5-Q5, each 2 leaves.
Caption title on p. 395. No imprint. Acts ratified December 1, 1766.
On p. 415 (Chap. XIII) is An Act, for appointing a Printer to this Province, by which James Davis was appointed for three years "from and after the passing of this Act."
NcU. NcSaM. NNB (bound with Vol. II of the *Collection* of 1765).

1767

NORTH CAROLINA (*Colony*). *Council.*
To | His Excellency | William Tryon, Esq; | His Majesty's Cap-

Anno Regni

GEORGII III. REGIS

MAGNÆ BRITANNIÆ, FRANCIÆ, & HIBERNIÆ,

QUINTO.

At an ASSEMBLY begun and held at WILMINGTON, *the Third Day of* FEBRUARY, *in the* Fourth *Year of the Reign of our Sovereign Lord* GEORGE *the* THIRD, *by the Grace of* GOD, *of* Great-Britain, France *and* Ireland, *King, Defender of the Faith,* &c. *and in the Year of our Lord,* One Thousand, Seven Hundred *and* Sixty-four; *and from thence continued, by Prorogations, to the* Third *Day of* MAY, *in the* Fifth *Year of the Reign of our said Sovereign Lord* GEORGE *the* THIRD, &c. *and in the Year of our Lord,* One Thousand, Seven Hundred *and* Sixty-five, *and then held at* NEWBERN; *being the* THIRD SESSION *of this present* ASSEMBLY.

The following LAWS were ENACTED.

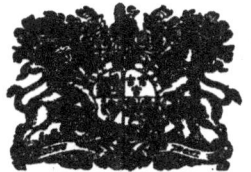

WILMINGTON:

Printed by ANDREW STEUART, Printer to the KING's MOST EXCELLENT MAJESTY. M,DCC,LXV.

tain-General, and Gover-|nor in Chief, in and over the Province of | North-Carolina; | the humble | Address | of his Majesty's | Council. | [Newbern: James Davis, 1767.] [52]
19 x 32 cm. Broadside.
No imprint.
PRO.

NORTH CAROLINA (*Colony*). *Governor* (*William Tryon*).
The | Speech | of his Excellency | William Tryon, Esq; | His Majesty's Captain-General, and Gover-|nor in Chief, in and over the Province of | North-Carolina; | To the General Assembly, held at Newbern, the | Fifth Day of December, One Thousand Seven Hundred and Sixty-seven. | [Newbern: James Davis, 1767.] [53]
19 x 32 cm. 3 p.
Caption title; no imprint.
PRO.

NORTH CAROLINA (*Colony*). *House of Assembly*.
To | his Excellency | William Tryon, Esq; | His Majesty's Captain-General, and Gover-|nor in Chief, in and over the Province of | North-Carolina; | the humble | Address | of the | House of Assembly. | [*Row of type ornaments*] | [Newbern: James Davis, 1767.] [54]
19 x 31 cm. 2 p.
Caption title; no imprint.
The Public Record Office copy has the MS endorsement: "Address of the Assembly of No. Carolina, to the Governor. In his Letter (No. 17) of 11. Decemr. 1767."
PRO.

1768

MICKLEJOHN, GEORGE.
On the Important Duty of Subjection to the | Civil Powers. | A | Sermon | Preached before his Excellency | William Tryon, Esquire, | Governor, and Commander in Chief of the | Province of North-Carolina, | and the | Troops raised to quell the late | Insurrection, | at | Hillsborough, in Orange County, | on Sunday

On the important Duty of SUBJECTION to the
CIVIL POWERS.

A

SERMON

Preached before his EXCELLENCY

WILLIAM TRYON, Efquire,
GOVERNOR, and Commander in Chief of the
Province of NORTH-CAROLINA,

AND THE

TROOPS raifed to quell the late

INSURRECTION,

AT

HILLSBOROUGH, in ORANGE County,

On SUNDAY *September* 25, 1768.

By GEO. MICKLEJOHN, S. T. D.

NEWBERN:

Printed by JAMES DAVIS,

M,DCC,LXVIII.

September 25, 1768. | [*Rule*] | By Geo. Micklejohn, S.T.D. | [*Rule*] | Newbern: | Printed by James Davis, | [*Rule*] | M,DCC,-LXVIII. [55]

14 x 18 cm. 15 p.

A loyalist's denunciation of the "Regulators" in North Carolina, based on the text "The powers that be are ordained of God." (Romans, xiii, 1-2.) On November 18, 1768, in a message to the Assembly, Governor Tryon said: "By the particular request of the Reverend Mr. Micklejohn, I desire leave in his behalf to present your House with one hundred copies of a sermon preached before the Troops at Hillsborough. The merit and beneficial tendency of this admirable discourse, gave general satisfaction to all who heard it delivered; a testimony it will undoubtedly receive from everyone who reads [it] with attention." (*Colonial Records*, VII, 939.) On December 3, acting on a recommendation from the Upper House, the House of Assembly agreed "that the Treasurers pay the expence of printing the sermon . . . sent to this House by His Excellency the Governor this session," and two days later the House addressed the governor, acknowledging the receipt of his message and the hundred copies of the sermon and notifying him that they had "Resolved that the Expense of printing the said Sermon be paid by the public." (*Colonial Records*, VII, 919-920, 939, 976, 983.) On March 20, 1769, Governor Tryon sent a copy of the sermon with a letter to Rev. Daniel Burton, secretary of the Society for the Propagation of the Gospel, London. (*Colonial Records*, VIII, 15.) Evans 10977 (not located). Weeks no. 33 (not located) knew of this only from the *Colonial Records;* Weeks 1896, p. 262, had the correct title, from *North Carolina University Magazine*, v. 4, 1855, p. 251.

See Boyd, *Some Eighteenth Century Tracts Concerning North Carolina*, p. 395-412, with reproduction of title page on p. 397.

NcHiC. DLC.

NORTH CAROLINA *(Colony). Governor (William Tryon).*
North-Carolina, ss. | George the Third, by the Grace of God, of Great-Britain, France, and Ireland, King, Defender of | the Faith, &c. | A Proclamation. | [12 *lines*] | William Tryon. | By His Excellency's Command, | Benj. Heron, Secretary. | God Save the King. | [Newbern: James Davis, 1768.] [56]

35 x 30 cm. Broadside.

No imprint.

Enjoining public officers to post tables of fees and accept no more than the authorized fees for their services. Dated at Brunswick, July 21, 1768.
PRO.

1769

NORTH CAROLINA (*Colony*). *Governor* (*William Tryon*).
The | Speech | of his Excellency | William Tryon, Esquire, | His Majesty's Captain General, Governor, and Commander in Chief, in | and over the Province of North-Carolina; | To the General Assembly, met at Newbern, the 23d Day of October, | One Thousand Seven Hundred and Sixty-Nine. | [Newbern: James Davis, 1769.] [57]
19 x 26 cm. 3 p.
Caption title; no imprint.
PRO.

NORTH CAROLINA (*Colony*). *House of Assembly*.
The | Journal | of the | House of Assembly. | [*Rule*] | North Carolina, ss. | At an Assembly begun and held at Newbern, the Twenty-third Day of Oc-|tober, in the Ninth Year of the Reign of our Sovereign Lord George | the Third, by the Grace of God, of Great-Britain, France and Ire-|land, King, Defender of the Faith, &c. and in the Year of our Lord | One Thousand Seven Hundred and Sixty-nine: Being the First Session | of this present Assembly. | [*Rule*] | [Newbern: James Davis, 1769.] [58]
19 x 31.5 cm. 20 p.
Caption title; no imprint.
The session lasted till November 6, 1769.
NcSaM.

1770

[HUSBANDS, HERMON]
An Impartial | Relation | of the | First Rise and Cause | of the | Recent·Differences, | in | Publick Affairs, | In the Province of North-Ca-|rolina; and of the past Tu-|mults and Riots that lately happened in that Province. | Containing most of the true and genuine | Copies of Letters, Messages and Remonstrances,

| between the Parties contending:—By which | any impartial Man may easily gather and see | the true Ground and Reason of the dissatisfaction | that universally reigns all over said Province in | a more or less Degree. | [2 *rules*] | Printed for the Compiler, [Newbern ?] 1770. [59]

9 x 15.5 cm. 104 p.

No imprint to show place or printer. It is by no means certain that this was printed in North Carolina, but Husbands, to whose authorship this tract is generally ascribed, was a resident of that province until after May, 1771. On the other hand, his activities with the Regulators, for which he was later expelled from the House of Assembly in December, 1770, and involved in many other difficulties, may have made it impossible for him to get James Davis, the province's official printer, to do this work even under the cloak of anonymity.

Husbands' name appears in contemporary records in a variety of spellings, but the most common form seems to be "Hermon," and this has been adopted in the index of the *Colonial Records*. The surname also is sometimes written "Husband."

See Boyd, *Some Eighteenth Century Tracts Concerning North Carolina*, p. 249-333, with reproduction of the title page on p. 251. Evans 11689. RPJCB.

[HUSBANDS, HERMON]
A Continuation of the | Impartial Relation | of the | First Rise and Cause | of the | Recent Differences, | in | Publick Affairs, | in the Province of North-Ca-|rolina, &c. | [*Rule*] | Second Part. | [*Rule*] | [*Type ornament*] | [*Double rule*] | Printed for the Author, | [Newbern ?] 1770. [60]

10.5 x 16 cm. 39 p.

By the same writer?: *A Fan for Fanning and a Touch-Stone to Tryon*, "containing an impartial account of the rise and progress of the so much talked of Regulation in North-Carolina, by Regulus." Boston, 1771. CSmH.

NORTH CAROLINA (*Colony*). *Governor* (*William Tryon*).
[A Plan for Keeping the Public Accounts. Newbern: James Davis, 1770.] [61]

Under date of November 30, 1769, Governor Tryon wrote to Lord Hills-

borough: "... I laid before both Houses a plan I had digested as nearly as possible conformable to that observed in Virginia, a copy of which is entered on the Journals of the upper House...." (*Colonial Records,* VIII, 152.) And on December 14, 1770, in a message to the House of Assembly, the Governor said: "I herewith send you a printed copy of a plan laid before the last Assembly for keeping the public accounts." (*Colonial Records,* VIII, 317.)
Weeks 1896, p. 262, no. 33a, dated this "1768 or 1769."

NORTH CAROLINA (*Colony*). *Laws, statutes, etc.*
[An Act for authorizing Presbyterian ministers, regularly called to any Congregation within this Province, to solemnize the Rites of Matrimony, under the regulations therein mentioned. Newbern: Printed by James Davis, 1770.] [62]
Title from Weeks 1896, p. 263, no. 33c, citing Rev. James Reed's letter of July 2, 1771, to the Society for the Propagation of the Gospel: "Lest by any accident the Governor's letter should have miscarried, I have sent you a printed copy of the act." (*Colonial Records,* IX, 5, 6.) This does not necessarily mean, of course, that this particular act was printed and issued separately.

1771

BURGWIN, JOHN, *compiler.*
North-Carolina. | A Table of the Number of Taxables in this Province from the Year 1748 inclusive, with the Taxes laid for each Year, and an Account of the Sums that should Arise by the Sinking Tax to the Year 1770. | [*Long line of type ornaments*] | Newbern: James Davis, 1771.] [63]
37.5 x 41 and 45.5 cm. Broadside, in 2 sheets. No imprint.
On January 25, 1771, by a resolution of the House of Assembly, John Burgwin was allowed three hundred pounds for his competent services in "collecting a compleat list of Taxables" and at the same time it was further "Resolved, that all real future necessary expences that may be incurred in printing and publishing six hundred copies of the state of the public accounts and the different Funds shall be allowed to him as a Claim on the Public." (*Colonial Records,* VIII, 379 and 461-462.)
See the reproduction in Boyd, *Some Eighteenth Century Tracts Concerning North Carolina,* at p. 416.
MHi.

NORTH CAROLINA (*Colony*). *Grand Jury.*
[Presentment of the Grand Jury, approving the proposal by Governor Tryon to go in person to suppress the insurgents, together with the association. Newbern, Printed by James Davis, 1771.] [64]
Governor Tryon wrote on April 12, 1771 to Earl Hillsborough: "Printed coppies of these have been circulated through the Province." See *Colonial Records*, VIII, 547.

NORTH CAROLINA (*Colony*). *House of Assembly.*
The | Journal | of the | House of Assembly. | North Carolina, ss. | At an Assembly begun and held at Newbern, the Fifth Day of December, in the Eleventh | Year of the Reign of our Sovereign Lord George the Third, by the Grace of God, | of Great Britain, France, and Ireland, King, Defender of the Faith, &c. and in the Year | of our Lord One Thousand Seven Hundred and Seventy; being the First Session of this | present Assembly. | [Newbern: James Davis, 1771.] [65]
21.5 x 32 cm. 24 (+ ?) p.
Caption title; no imprint.
There seem to have been two issues of the journal of this session. In the copy here described, the text is consecutive, but p. 24 is followed by p. 21-74 of what is, apparently, the issue described below as no. 66. On p. 24 of this issue the date changes from December 31, 1770, to January 1, 1771. The caption titles of the two issues differ in typographical make-up.
NcSaM.

NORTH CAROLINA (*Colony*). *House of Assembly.*
The | Journal | of the | House of Assembly. | [*Rule*] | North-Carolina, sc. | At an Assembly began [*sic*] and held at Newbern, the Fifth Day of December, in the Eleventh | Year of the Reign of our Sovereign Lord George the Third, by the Grace of God, of | Great Britain, France, and Ireland, King, Defender of the Faith, &c. and in the Year of | our Lord One Thousand Seven Hundred and Seventy; being the first Session of this present |

Assembly. | [*Rule*] | [Newbern: Printed by James Davis, 1771.]
19 x 32.5 cm. 74 p.   [66]
Caption title; no imprint.
The session ended January 26, 1771.
NcU. NcSaM (p. 21-74; see no. 65).

1773

NORTH CAROLINA (*Colony*). *House of Assembly.*
The | Journal | of the | House of Assembly. | North Carolina, ss. | At an Assembly, begun and held at Newbern, the Twenty Fifth Day of January, in | the Thirteenth Year of the Reign of our Sovereign Lord George the Third, by the | Grace of God, of Great-Britain, France, and Ireland, King | Defender of the Faith, | &c. and in the Year of our Lord One Thousand Seven Hundred and Seventy three; | being the First Session of this present Assembly. [*Rule*] | Newbern: James Davis, 1773.]   [67]
19.5 x 31.5 cm. 67 p.
Caption title; no imprint.
The session lasted till March 6, 1773.
NcSaM.

NORTH CAROLINA (*Colony*). *House of Assembly.*
The | Journal | of the House of Assembly, | of the Province of | North Carolina. | At an Assembly, begun and held at | Newbern, the Fourth Day of December, in the Fourteenth Year | of the Reign of our Sovereign Lord George the Third, by | the Grace of God, of Great-Britain, France and Ireland, | King, Defender of the Faith, &c. and in the Year of our Lord | 1773; being the first Session of this present Assembly. | [*Rule*] | [*Royal arms*] | [*Rule*] | Newbern: | Printed by James Davis, Printer to the Honourable the House | of Assembly. MDCCLXXIII.   [68]
22.5 x 28.5 cm. 8+ p.
The session lasted till December 21, 1773.
NcSaM (only 8 p. preserved).

NORTH CAROLINA (*Colony*). *Laws, statutes, etc.*
A | Complete Revisal | of all the | Acts | of | Assembly, | of the

Province of | North-Carolina, | now in force and use. | [*Line of type ornaments*] | Together | with the title of all such laws as | are obsolete, expired, or repealed. | [*Line of type ornaments*] | With | marginal notes and references, and an | exact table to the whole. | [*Line of type ornaments*] | Newbern: | Printed by James Davis, Printer to the Honourable the House of Assembly. MDCCLXXIII. [69]

19.5 x 29.5 cm. 2 preliminary leaves, x, 566, [9] p.

Proposals for printing this *Revisal* by subscription were published in the *North-Carolina Gazette* of November 10, 1769: "To the Public. As the first edition of the late revisal of the laws [1764] . . . is intirely sold off, that alone would be a sufficient reason, were there no other, for a second; as there is still a great demand for them, to supply the numerous inhabitants of this extensive province; But when the public are made acquainted, that by the expiration of a great number of temporary acts; the repeal of others; and the late re-enaction of the acts for establishing superior and inferior courts; for regulating and directing the duty of sheriffs; and many other public acts, the whole plan and system of the late revisal is altered; they will no longer doubt of the expediency of a second revisal at this time. Upon these considerations the publisher undertakes it, . . . and would esteem it a particular favour in gentlemen that may have marked any errors in the late edition, to communicate the same, as they may be corrected, and the work rendered more compleat.

"By a revisal of the laws, the public are not to understand, as in propriety of speech they might, an entire correction of the many voluminous acts of assembly of this province, and the same reduced to a narrow code or system; this is a work of time, expence, and labour, and only belongs to the legislature, or persons properly qualified, by them authorized; and perhaps may not be undertaken while the province groans under its present distresses; The present plan is only to arrange the several acts that have been enacted from time to time, in the order in which they were passed; to mark the repealed, expired, or obsolete laws, and only insert the titles; and, as many laws are repealed in part only, to leave out the repealed part, or what comes within the purview of the repealing act, and only insert the clauses left in force, — This, with humble submission to the legislature, is a way of repealing that introduces infinite confusion in our laws, and renders a compleat knowledge of them very laborious . . . .

"These proposals were published some time ago, and the books were to have been delivered this fall [1769]; the work was accordingly carried

A COMPLETE REVISAL

OF ALL THE

ACTS

OF

ASSEMBLY,

OF THE PROVINCE OF

NORTH-CAROLINA,

NOW IN FORCE AND USE.

TOGETHER
WITH THE TITLES OF ALL SUCH LAWS AS
ARE OBSOLETE, EXPIRED, OR REPEALED.

WITH
MARGINAL NOTES AND REFERENCES, AND AN
EXACT TABLE TO THE WHOLE.

NEWBERN:
Printed by JAMES DAVIS, Printer to the Honourable the House of
Assembly. MDCCLXXIII.

on, every sheet of it was lost in the ruins of the Printing-Office, which was totally swept away in the late storm; also the list of subscribers' names that had been returned. They are therefore published again, in order to notify the misfortune, and to request the favour of those gentlemen that have already subscribed, to transmit their names again to the Printing Office." The terms of the proposals called for a work in one large quarto volume to contain about 600 pages, neatly bound, with the subscribers' names printed in the books, at 40 shillings a copy.

As to the "late storm" in which Davis lost his printing office, a letter from Newbern to Governor Tryon dated September 19, 1769, relates of the destruction on the night of September 7th: "Mr. Davis's house a mere wreck, his printing office broke to pieces, his papers destroyed and types buried in the sand, his desk stove, and what money he had with all his private papers entirely lost." (*Colonial Records,* VIII, 74.)

Weeks no. 34. Evans 12904 (not located).

CSmH. NcAS. NcD. Nc-Law. NcU. DLC. M. MB. MH-L. MHi. NHi. NIC. NNB. NNC. PHi. Cotten.

1774

DAVIS, JAMES.
The | Office and Authority | of a | Justice of Peace. | And also, | The Duty of Sheriffs, Coroners, Con-|stables, Churchwardens, Overseers | of Roads, and other Officers. | Together with | Precedents of Warrants, Judgments, Execu- | tions, and other legal Process, issuable by Ma- | gistrates within their several Jurisdictions, in Cases | Civil and Criminal, with the Method of Judicial | Proceedings before Justices of the Peace out of Sessi- | ons. Also some Directions for their Conduct within | their County Courts. | To which is added, | An Appendix. | Containing many useful Precedents, and Directions | for the Execution of them. | Collected from the Common and Statute Laws of | England, and the Acts of Assembly of this Province, | and adapted to our Constitution and Practice. | [*Line of ornaments*] | By J. Davis, Esq; one of his Majesty's Justices of | the Peace for the County of Craven. | [*Line of ornaments*] | Newbern: | Printed by James Davis, M,DCC,LXXIV. [70]

12 x 19 cm. 2 leaves, 404, [3] p.

THE OFFICE and AUTHORITY OF A JUSTICE of PEACE.

AND ALSO,

The Duty of SHERIFFS, CORONERS, CONSTABLES, CHURCHWARDENS, OVERSEERS of ROADS, and other Officers.

TOGETHER WITH

PRECEDENTS of WARRANTS, JUDGMENTS, EXECUTIONS, and other legal PROCESS, issuable by Magistrates within their several Jurisdictions, in Cases Civil and Criminal, with the Method of Judicial Proceedings before Justices of the Peace out of Sessions. Also some Directions for their Conduct within their County Courts.

To which is added,

An APPENDIX.

Containing many useful PRECEDENTS, and Directions for the Execution of them.

Collected from the Common and Statute Laws of *England*, and the Acts of Assembly of this Province, and adapted to our Constitution and Practice.

By J. DAVIS, Esq; one of his Majesty's Justices of the Peace for the County of *Craven*.

NEWBERN:

Printed by JAMES DAVIS. M,DCC,LXXIV.

Library of Congress copy defective in that signature E is not signed and has its pages numbered 27, 26, 27, 26, 31, 30, 30, 30 — pages 27, 26, 31 and 30 being duplicated and the other pages of the signature missing. Other copies have signature E signed with all its pages present and in their correct order.

Advertised in the *North-Carolina Gazette* of February 21, 1775: "This day is published, beautifully printed, on an entire new Type, and good Paper, and to be sold at the Printing Office in Newbern, neatly bound in Law Binding. Price Two Dollars."

Weeks no. 35 (not located). Evans 13236 (not located).
DLC. NcAS. NcD. NcU. Cotten.

The First Book of the American | Chronicles of the Times. | [Newbern: James Davis, 1774.]   [71]
11 x 17.5 cm. 15 p.
Caption title. Imprint on p. 15: Newbern: Printed by J. Davis. 1774.
Advertised in the *North-Carolina Gazette* of February 24, 1775: "Just published, and to be sold at the Printing Office, and by most of the Storekeepers in Town and Country, (Price Eight Coppers) . . . A Work of so much Humour, that upwards of 3000 Copies thereof were sold in a few days at Philadelphia."
Evans 13107. Sabin 24404 (not located).
RPJCB.

NEWBERN (*North Carolina*). *Inhabitants.*
Newbern, August 9, 1774. | To the Freeholders of Craven | County. | Gentlemen, | This Day a considerable Number of the Inhabitants of New-|bern met at the Court-House, . . . | [12 *lines*] | We are, Gentlemen, your obedient Servants, | [9 *names in 2 columns*] | Newbern: James Davis, 1774.]   [72]
14 x 14 cm. (lower portion cut away). Broadside.
Among the names printed at the end, that of James Davis is first. The broadside give notice that the meeting "appointed Abner Nash and Isaac Edwards, Esqrs. Deputies, to act for them at the general Meeting to be held here on the 25th Instant, for the Purposes of taking into Consideration the present alarming State of British America, and the late Acts of Parliament relating to the Port of Boston and Province of Massachusetts-Bay," and called a meeting at Newbern on the 20th of August for the inhabitants of Craven County, to "instruct their Members of Assembly,

or such other Persons as they may chuse, to represent them in the said general Meeting."

The lower portion of this broadside, or handbill, has been cut off in such a way as to indicate that perhaps one of the list of names at the end was intentionally removed.

There is no imprint, but James Davis was unquestionably the printer.
PRO.

NORTH CAROLINA (*Colony*). *House of Assembly.*
[The Journal of the House of Assembly. At an Assembly, begun and held ... on the Second Day of March, in ... the Year of our Lord One Thousand Seven Hundred and Seventy Four; ... Newbern: James Davis, 1774.] [73]
22.5 x 31.5 cm. 49 p.
Caption title ? No imprint at end.
The session lasted till March 25, 1774.
NcSaM (defective — p. 21-49 only).

NORTH CAROLINA (*Colony*). *Laws, statutes, etc.*
The | Acts | of | Assembly | of the Province of | North-Carolina, | Passed | At an Assembly, began [*sic*] and held | at Newbern, the Second Day of March, in the Fourteenth | Year of the Reign of our Sovereign Lord George the | Third, by the Grace of God, of Great-Britain, France, | and Ireland, King, Defender of the Faith, &c. and in | the Year of our Lord One Thousand Seven Hundred and | Seventy Four; being the Second Session of this present | Assembly. | [*Rule*] | [*Royal arms*] | [*Rule*] | Newbern: | Printed by James Davis, Printer to the Honourable the | House of Assembly. MDCCLXXIV. [74]
22 x 32 cm. Title page (verso blank) and p. 567-612. Signatures Rrrr (on p. 567) -Eeeee, each 2 leaves (last leaf blank).
Caption title on p. 567: [*Headband of type ornaments*] | Anno Regni | Georgii III. | Regis | Magnæ Britanniæ, Franciæ, & Hiberniæ, | Decimo Quarto. | [*Rule*] | At an Assembly, began [*sic*] and held at Newbern, the Second Day of | March, in the Fourteenth Year of the Reign of our Sovereign Lord | George the Third, by the Grace of God, of Great-Britain, France, | and Ireland, King, Defender of the Faith, &c. and in the Year of

our | Lord One Thousand Seven Hundred and Seventy Four; being the | Second Session of this Assembly. | [*Rule*].
Acts ratified March 19, 1774. On p. 606 (Chap. XXI) is An Act for further continuing An Act, intituled, An Act for appointing a Printer to this Province. See *Colonial Records*, XXIII, p. 971.
Evans 13504.
NcU.

WILMINGTON DISTRICT (*N. C.*). *Inhabitants.*
At a General Meeting of the Inhabitants of the District of Wilmington in the | Province of North-Carolina, held at the Town of Wilmington | July 21st, 1774. | William Hooper, Esq; Chairman. | Resolved ... | [Wilmington: Adam Boyd, 1774.]
15 x 19 cm. Broadside. [75]
No imprint.
Resolutions appointing a committee to prepare a circular letter to the other counties of North Carolina and proposing the convening of all the American colonies to meet in Philadelphia.
PRO.

WILMINGTON (*North Carolina*). *Committee of Correspondence.*
Gentlemen, | At this Conjuncture of British Politics when the Liberty and Property of North- | American Subjects are at Stake, ... | [22*lines*] | [Wilmington: Adam Boyd, 1774.] [76]
14.5 x 19 cm. Broadside.
Circular letter sent out by the committee appointed at the meeting at Wilmington on July 21, 1774, transmitting a copy of the resolutions adopted at that meeting (no. 75, above). The copy described was addressed in handwriting "To The Freeholders of Craven County" and was signed with the autographs of James Moore and three others. It was endorsed upon receipt in London "In Govr. Martin's (No. 26) of 1st Septr. 1774."
The letter requests that the community addressed "would send the Members, already by you elected, to represent you in the General Assembly, or such other Persons whom you shall approve of to appear as your Deputies at the Court-House of Johnson County, on the 20th Day of August next, possessed of the Sentiments of those in whose Behalf they attend, and with full Power to express it as obligatory upon the future Conduct of the Inhabitants of this Province; and, then and there, to consult and determine

At a General Meeting of the Inhabitants of the District of Wilmington in the Province of NORTH-CAROLINA, held at the Town of Wilmington July 21st, 1774.

WILLIAM HOOPER, Esq; Chairman.

RESOLVED, That Col. James Moore, John Ancrum, Fred. Jones, Samuel Ashe, Robert Howe, Robert Hogg, Francis Clayton and Archibald Maclaine, Esqrs. be a Committee to prepare a circular Letter to the several Counties of this Province, expressive of the Sense of the Inhabitants of this district with respect to the several Acts of Parliament lately made for the oppression of our Sister Colony of the Massachusetts-Bay, for having exerted itself in defence of the constitutional Rights of America.

RESOLVED, That it will be highly expedient that the several Counties of this Province should send Deputies to attend a General Meeting at Johnston Court House on the 20th Day of August next, then & there to debate upon the present alarming State of British America, and in concert with the other Colonies, to adopt and prosecute such Measures as will most effectually tend to avert the Miseries which threaten us.

RESOLVED, That we are of Opinion, in order to effect an uniform Plan for the Conduct of all North-America, that it will be necessary that a general Congress be held, and that Deputies should there be present from the several Colonies, fully informed of the Sentiments of those in whose behalf they appear, that such Regulations may then be made as will tend most effectually to produce an alteration in the British Policy, and to bring about a Change honourable and beneficial to all America.

RESOLVED, That we have the most grateful Sense of the spirited Conduct of Maryland, Virginia, and all other the Northern Provinces, and also the Province of South-Carolina, upon this interesting Occasion, and will with our Purses and Persons, concur with them in all legal Measures that may be conceived by the Colonies in general, as most expedient in order to bring about the End which we all so earnestly wish for.

RESOLVED, That it is the Opinion of this Meeting, that Philadelphia will be the most proper Place for holding the American Congress, and the 20th of September the most suitable Time: but in this we submit our own to the general Convenience of the other Colonies.

RESOLVED, That we consider the Cause of the Town of Boston as the common Cause of British America, and as suffering in Defence of the Rights of the Colonies in general; and that therefore we have, in Proportion to our Abilities, sent a Supply of Provisions for the indigent Inhabitants of that Place, thereby to express our Sympathy in their Distress, and as an Earnest of our sincere Intentions, to contribute by every Means in our Power to alleviate their Distress, and to induce them to maintain, with Prudence and Firmness, the glorious Cause in which they at present suffer.

what may be necessary to the general Welfare of America and of this Province."
There is no imprint, but Adam Boyd, publisher of the Wilmington *Cape-Fear Mercury,* was undoubtedly the printer.
PRO.

1775

CRAVEN COUNTY (*N. C.*). *Committee.*
At a Meeting of the Committee | for the County of Craven, and | Town of Newbern, on the 4th | Day of March, 1775. | Resolved, that at this critical Juncture it becomes the Duty | of this Committee to remind their Constituents, that several | important Rule and Regulations, established by the Gene-|ral Congress ... | [Newbern: James Davis, 1775.]   [77]
18 x 30 cm. Broadside.
No imprint.
Exhortation to all Americans to unite and support the General Congress; signed at end by R. Cogdell and twelve others, including James Davis.
PRO.

CRAVEN COUNTY (*N. C.*) *Committee.*
Proceedings of the Committee | for the Town of Newbern, and | County of Craven, May 31, 1775. | Circular Letter to the several Committees of this Province. | [Newbern: James Davis, 1775.]
21.5 x 31 cm. 4 p.   [78]
Caption title; no imprint. On p. 2 is the heading: A Circular Letter to the Committees in the several Districts and Parishes of South Carolina. Charlestown, April 27, 1775. And on p. 4 the heading: Association. The latter is a proposed association of the people of Newbern and of Craven County to "Assert our Rights as Men ... "
NcSaM.

CRISIS, THE.
[The Crisis. A Periodical Paper lately published in London, in 8 Numbers. Newbern: Printed by James Davis, 1775.]   [79]
8vo. 64 p.
Advertised in the *North-Carolina Gazette* of July 14, 1775: "This Day is published, and to be sold at the Printing Office in Newbern, Price 1s. 6d."

At a Meeting of the COMMITTEE *for the County of* CRAVEN, *and Town of* NEWBERN, *on the* 4th *Day of* March, 1775.

RESOLVED, that at this critical Juncture it becomes the Duty of this Committee to remind their Constituents, that several important Rules and Regulations, established by the General Congress, have now lately taken Place; and they hereby beg Leave earnestly to exhort them, as they regard the future Welfare of themselves and their Posterity, to remain firm and steady in the common Cause of Liberty, and that they testify the same by paying a sacred Regard to those Rules, as the only Means left, under Divine Providence, of delivering *America* from the cruel Hand of arbitrary Power: We, of the Committee, at the same Time observe, with inexpressible Joy, that the People of *New-York* remain firm in the good Cause of Liberty, notwithstanding every Art that a corrupt Ministry, and a Set of despicable Scribblers under them, could invent and put in Practice, to create a Division of political Sentiments in that Province; and that they have lately obliged Two Ships, richly laden with *British* Goods, to leave their Port, and return to the Place from whence they came, agreeable to the Articles of Association recommended by the General Congress, which all are equally bound, by every Tie of Honour, mutual Faith, and personal Security, to observe and support, for the arbitrary Designs of Parliament appear no longer under Disguise---the Standard of its Tyranny is now erected in this once happy Land; and a melancholy Sample have they afforded us, of what we may expect in future from their Justice and Equity, if we submit to their Edicts already past; for she not only assumes the Right of taxing us at Pleasure, and, in short, of making Laws to bind us in all Cases whatsoever; but, to crown the Whole, she has past a Law for transporting us like Felons occasionally over Sea, to be tried, condemned and punished, in Case we should at any Time murmur at our Hardships, or prove otherwise obnoxious to Men in Power; and to carry this most cruel Scheme of Tyranny into Execution, we find the Towns of our Fellow Countrymen to the Northward infested with Armies, and their Ports and Harbours with Fleets. Be sensible, O *Americans!* of your Danger; let that unite you together as one Man, and cease not to implore the great Disposer of all Things to assist and crown with Success the Councils of the General Congress.

R. Cogdell,
Abner Nash,
Richard Blackledge,
Farnifold Green,
John Fonveille,
James Davis,
Edmond Hatch,

James Coor,
Jacob Johnston,
Jacob Blount,
Joseph Leech,
Alex. Gaston,
William Bryan.

The advertisement describes the publication thus: "It is a true Portrait of the present Times, and wrote with great Freedom. It has been consigned to the Flames by the present pious Parliament, the common Hangman having burnt it in several Places in London by their order."
See Evans 13901, 13911, 13921, 13930, 13939, 13948, 13957, 13964.

T. J. Emery, | Gives this public Notice to his Friends and Customers, that he has just imported from England, ... | ... a very large and complete Assortment of European | Goods, which he is now selling at his new Store in Newbern ... | [2 *lines, followed by list of goods in* 4 *columns*] | Said Emery has also for Sale ... | [1 *line*] | [Newbern ? 1755 ?] [80]
28 x 45 cm. Broadside.
This broadside was used by Emery as wrapping paper for paper money. A date in handwriting on the reverse, Jan. 30, 1776, signed by T. J. Emery, makes it seem likely that the broadside was printed in Newbern in 1775 or in January, 1776.
NN (2 copies).

HARVEY, JOHN.
Advertisement. | [*Rule*] | Perquimans County, Feb. 11, 1775. | The respective Counties and Towns in this Colony are | requested to elect Delegates to represent them in Con-|vention, who are desired to meet at the Town of Newbern on | Monday the 3d Day of April next. | John Harvey, Moderator. | [Newbern: James Davis, 1775.] [81]
15 x 10 cm. Broadside.
No imprint.
PRO.

NORTH CAROLINA (*Colony*). *Governor* (*Josiah Martin*).
North-Carolina, ss. | By his Excellency | Josiah Martin, Esq. | Captain-General, Governor, and Commander in Chief, in and over the | said Province. | A Proclamation . | [45 *lines*] | Given under my Hand, and the Great Seal of the said Province, | at Newbern, | the 10th Day of February, Anno | Dom. 1775, and in

the 15th Year of his Majesty's Reign. | Jo. Martin. | God save the King. | By his Excellency's Command, | James Parratt, D. Sec. | [Newbern: James Davis, 1775.] [82]
32 x 44 cm. Broadside.
No imprint.
Forbidding Richard Henderson to establish a colony for undesirable citizens on land acquired by treaty of purchase from the Cherokees.
PRO.

NORTH CAROLINA (*Colony*). *Governor* (*Josiah Martin*).
North-Carolina. | By His Excellency | Josiah Martin, Esq. | His Majesty's Captain-General, Governor, and Commander in Chief, in and over | the said Province. | A Proclamation. | Whereas I have received certain information, that sundry ill-disposed | Persons have been, and are still going about the country of Brunswick, and other counties of this province industriously | propagating false, seditious, and scandalous reports, derogatory to the honour and justice of the King and his govern-|ment .... | [*At end*]: Given, under my Hand, and the Great Seal of the said Province, at Fort Johnston, | this Sixteenth Day of June, 1775, and in the Fifteenth Year of his Majesty's Reign. | Josiah Martin. | By his Excellency's Command, | Alexander Maclean pro James Biggleston, D. Secretary. | God Save the King. | [Newbern: James Davis, 1775.] [83]
21 x 33 cm. Broadside.
No imprint.
Exhorting the inhabitants of North Carolina to loyalty to the crown.
PRO.

NORTH CAROLINA (*Colony*). *Provincial Congress.*
The | Journal | of the | Proceedings | of the | Provincial Congress, | of North-Carolina. | Held at Hillsborough on the 20th Day of | August, 1775. | [*Filet*] | Published by Authority. | [*Filet*] | Newbern: | Printed by James Davis, Printer to the Honourable | the House of Assembly. MDCCLXXV. [84]
16 x 20.5 cm. 40 p.

The session lasted to September 10, 1775.
Advertised in the *North-Carolina Gazette* of October 6, 1775: "This day is published, and to be sold at the Printing Office in Newbern, Price 2/6..."
Weeks no. 37 ("there is a printed copy ... in the Public Record Office in London"). Evans 14354.
DLC. NcSaM. NcU (lacking last leaf). RPJCB.

PITT, WILLIAM, 1st *Earl of Chatham*.
[The Speech of the Right Honourable the Earl of Chatham, in the House of Lords, January 20, 1775, on a Motion for an Address to his Majesty, to give immediate Orders for removing his Troops from Boston forthwith, in order to quiet the minds, and take away the apprehensions of his good subjects in America. Newbern: Printed by James Davis, 1775.] [85]
Advertised in the *North-Carolina Gazette* of June 30, 1775, as "just published, and to be sold at the Printing Office, price Eight Pence." The fact of its printing at Newbern is further confirmed by this further note in the same issue: "In No. 322 of this Paper we gave what then appeared to be Lord Chatham's speech. But to preserve the Purity of that great Man's Thoughts on American Liberty, an exact Copy of the original Speech, taken down as it was spoken in the House of Lords, has been transmitted to Philadelphia in Manuscript, and there published in an elegant Pamphlet. From that Copy the same is now published here, and ought by every true American to be preserved, as the liveliest Picture ever drawn of his Rights and Liberties, invaded by a wicked and tyrannical Ministry."
The Philadelphia issue was printed by John Dunlap, 1775.

PRESBYTERIAN CHURCH. *Synod of Philadelphia*.
[An Address to the Ministers and Presbyterian Congregations in North-Carolina. Wilmington: Adam Boyd, 1775.] [86]
Weeks, 1896, p. 263, no. 36a, records this as a "hypothetical title based on *Colonial Records*, X, 188," and suggests it as probable that it was first printed in Boyd's *Cape Fear Mercury* and then reprinted for presentation to the provincial congress. The cited passage in *Colonial Records* reads: "Sept. 2, 1775. Mr. Boyd laid before the Congress two hundred pastoral letters from the Synod of Philadelphia addressed to the Inhabitants of

THE
JOURNAL
OF THE

PROCEEDINGS

OF THE

PROVINCIAL CONGRESS,

OF NORTH-CAROLINA.

Held at HILLSBOROUGH on the 20th Day of
AUGUST, 1775.

PUBLISHED BY AUTHORITY.

NEWBERN:
Printed by JAMES DAVIS, Printer to the Honourable
the House of Assembly. MDCCLXXV.

this province, which were dispersed among the members. Resolved, that the said Adam Boyd be allowed the sum of ...... Proclamation money to be paid by the public Treasurers or either of them, and be allowed in their accounts with the Public."
The address, dated at Philadelphia, July 10, 1775, has been reprinted in *Colonial Records,* X, 222-228.

UNITED STATES. *Continental Congress.*
[Extracts from the Votes and Proceedings of the American Continental Congress, held at Philadelphia, on the fifth day of September, 1774, containing the Bill of Rights, a List of Grievances, Occasional Resolves, the Association, an Address to the People of Great Britain, and a Memorial to the Inhabitants of the British American Colonies. Also the Letter to the Inhabitants of Quebec, and General Gage's Answer to the Letter sent him by the General Congress. Newbern: Printed by James Davis, 1775.]
[87]
Advertised in the *North-Carolina Gazette* of February 24, 1775, as "just published, and to be sold at the Printing Office, in Newbern, price two Shillings."

UNITED STATES. *Continental Congress. North Carolina Delegates.*
To the Committees of the several Towns and Counties of the Province of North-Caro-|lina, appointed for the Purpose of carrying into Execution the Resolves of the Continental | Congress. | Gentlemen, | When the Liberties of a People are invaded, ... | [Newbern ? 1775.] [88]
19 x 29 cm. 2 p.
No imprint.
Exhorting the people of North Carolina to awake to their present danger and to train and equip a militia. Signed at end: William Hopper, Joseph Hewes, Richard Caswell, Philadelphia, June 19, 1775. Though the letter was dated from Philadelphia, I am inclined to believe it was printed in North Carolina, probably at Newbern.
This copy was endorsed upon its receipt in London: "In Govr. Martin's (No. 39) of 28 August 1775."
PRO.

1776

NORTH CAROLINA (*Colony*). *Governor (Josiah Martin*).
North-Carolina, St. | By His Excellency Josiah Martin, His Majesty's Captain General, Governor and Commander in Chief | in and over the said Province. | A Proclamation. | [*85 lines*] | Given under My Hand, and the Great Seal of the said Province on board the Snow Peggy, in Cape-Fear River, this Seventh Day of April 1776, and in the | Sixteenth Year of His Majesty's Reign. (Signed) Josiah Martin. | God save the King. | Extract from the Votes of the House of Commons of 29th November, 1775. | [*23 lines*]. | [1776.] [89]
32.5 x 41.5 cm. Broadside. No imprint.
Calls upon his Majesty's subjects who are in rebellion to return to their allegiance, promising, in addition to regular pay, free grants of land exempt from quit-rent for ten years to those who bear arms to suppress the rebellion; and declares martial law in North Carolina.
Evans 14949.
DLC (MS Div.).

NORTH CAROLINA. *Provincial Congress.*
The | Journal | of the | Proceedings | of the | Provincial Congress | of North-Carolina, | Held at Halifax on the 4th Day of April, 1776. | [*Filet*] | Published by Authority. | [*Filet*] | Newbern: | Printed by James Davis, Printer to the Honourable the House of Assembly. | MDCCLXXVI. [90]
18 x 22 cm. 45 p.
The congress continued to May 14, 1776.
Weeks no. 38 (from Sabin 55631). Evans 14948. Reprinted in 1831.
DLC (lacking last leaf). *NcSaM*.

1777

[The Manual Exercise, as ordered by the British King in the Year 1764. With the Manner of Priming and Loading, and the Position of each Rank in Firings. And the Method of performing the Firings, Evolutions, &c. at Reviews and Field Days. To which is added, the Articles of War of the Continental Army. Newbern? James Davis? 1777.] [91]

[85]

Advertised in the *North-Carolina Gazette* of July 4, 1777, as "also to be sold at the said Office." Such a work was needed by the military and would be quite appropriate for local printing, but it is possible the copies here advertised for sale had been imported from a city farther northward. Evans 15359 records an edition by Hugh Gaine, New York, 1777, but this may have been Gaine's 1775 edition readvertised in the *Mercury,* no. 1360 (P. L. Ford, *Journals of Hugh Gaine, Printer,* vol. 1, p. 146). No other edition of 1777 seems to be recorded, and particularly no edition containing "the articles of war of the Continental Army."

There were 1774 editions at Boston, Newburyport, New Haven, and Providence (Evans 13319-13323); 1775 at Baltimore, Lancaster, New York, Norwich, Philadelphia (2), Williamsburg (2), Wilmington, Del. (Evans 14101-14109); and 1776 at Philadelphia (Evans 14797).

NORTH CAROLINA. *Laws, statutes, etc.*
The | Acts | of | Assembly | of the State of | North Carolina. | Passed | At a General Assembly | begun and held at Newbern on the Eighth Day of April, | in the Year of our Lord One Thousand Seven Hundred | and Seventy Seven, and in the First Year of the Indepen-|dence of the said State: Being the First Session of this | Assembly. | [*Line of type ornaments*] | [*Second line of type ornaments*] | Newbern: | Printed by James Davis. MDCCL-XXVII. [92]

19.5 x 30.5 cm. [2], 38 p. Title in border of type ornaments.

The wording of the title page is repeated as a caption title on p. 1, under a headband of type ornaments.

Advertised in the *North-Carolina Gazette* of October 17, 1777, as "Just published, and to be sold at the Printing Office, Price One Dollar." The advertisement goes on to explain: "Mr. Pinkney, who was appointed Printer to this State in April last, being dead, and no Prospect of the State's being able to get their Laws printed, Mr. Davis informs the Public, that he has undertaken this necessary Work, and will dispatch them to the several Counties as soon as possible." These Acts had previously been advertised in the same newspaper of October 3 and October 10 as "in the press." The "just published" continued to appear in the same advertisement as late as February, 1778.

The acts of this session were ratified May 9, 1777.

Weeks no. 40. Evans 15487.

DLC. NcD. NcSaM. NcU (title page defective). *PHi.*

NORTH CAROLINA. *Provincial Congress.*
The | Journal | of the | Proceedings | of the | Provincial Congress | of North-Carolina, | Held at Halifax the 12th Day of November, 1776. | Together with | The Declaration of Rights, | Constitution, & Ordinances | of Congress. | [*Filet*] | Published by Authority. | [*Filet*] | Newbern: | Printed by James Davis, Printer to the Honourable the General | Assembly. MDCCLXXVII.
12.5 x 18 cm. 84 p. [93]
The congress continued to December 23, 1776.
Weeks no. 39 (from Sabin 55632). Evans 15489.
DLC. NcSaM (lacking p. 81-84). MBAt.

UNITED STATES. *Articles of Confederation.*
Articles | of | Confederation | and | Perpetual Union | between the | states | of | New Hampshire, Massachusetts Bay, Rhode Island and Provi-|dence Plantations, Connecticut, New York, New Jersey, | Pennsylvania, Delaware, Maryland, Virginia, North-Ca-|rolina, South Carolina, and Georgia. | [*Double rule*] | Lancaster, Printed. | Newbern: Re-printed by James Davis, | MDCCLXXVII. [94]
18 x 29 cm. 9 p.
Advertised in the *North-Carolina Gazette* of January 2, 1778, as "Just published and to be sold at the Printing Office in Newbern, price half a dollar .... lately published by order of Congress, and absolutely necessary to be had by every person who wishes well to this union, and wants to know how the glorious Fabrick of this new world is to be regulated."
Weeks no. 42. See Sabin 2142.
DLC.

1778

DYCHE, THOMAS.
[Dyche's Spelling Book; or a Guide to the English Tongue. In Two Parts. The first, proper for Beginners, showing a natural and easy method, to pronounce and express both common words, and proper names; in which particular care is had to show the accent, for preventing vicious pronunciation. The Second, for such as are advanced to some ripeness of judgment, containing

[87]

observations on the sound of letters and Diphthongs; rules for the true division of syllables, and the use of capitals, stops, and marks: With large tables of abbreviation, and distinctions of words; and several alphabets of copies for young writers. To which is now added, An Appendix, containing many additional lessons, in prose and verse; First, in words of one syllable only; and then mix'd with words of two, three, four, five, six, and seven syllables. Newbern: Printed by James Davis, 1778?] [95]
Advertised in the *North-Carolina Gazette* of Nov. 7 and 14, 1778: "In the Press, and in a few weeks will be published, price bound Two Dollars and a Half." It is possible, of course, that it never appeared.
Weeks no. 49. Evans 15789.

NORTH CAROLINA. *General Assembly. House of Commons.*
The | Journal | of the | House of Commons. | [*Row of type ornaments*] | State of North-Carolina. | At a General Assembly, begun and held at Newbern on the 14th Day of April, in the Year of our Lord 1778, and in the se-|cond Year of the Independence of said State: Being the first | Session of this Assembly. | [Newbern: James Davis, 1778.] [96]
20 x 30 cm. 36 (+?) p.
Caption title; no imprint.
The session lasted to May 1, 1778.
DLC (complete ?)

NORTH CAROLINA. *General Assembly. House of Commons.*
The | Journal | of the | House of Commons. | [*Rule*] | State of North-Carolina. | At a General Assembly, begun and held at Hillsborough on the 8th Day of August, | in the Year of our Lord 1778, and in the third Year of the Independence of the said State: | Being the second Session of this Assembly. | [Newbern: Printed by James Davis, 1778.] [97]
18.5 x 28 cm. 24+ p.
Caption title; no imprint.
NcU (lacking all after p. 24).

NORTH CAROLINA. *Laws, statutes, etc.*
The | Acts | of | Assembly | of the state of | North Carolina. | Passed | at a General Assembly | begun and held at Newbern on the Fifteenth Day of | November, in the Year of Our Lord One Thousand Seven | Hundred and Seventy Seven, and in the Second Year of | the Independence of the said State: Being the Second | Session of this Assembly. | [*Line of type ornaments*] | Published by Authority. | [*Line of type ornaments*] | Newbern: | Printed by James Davis, Printer to the Honourable the | General Assembly. MDCCLXXVIII. [98]
20 x 32.5 cm. 84 p.
Advertised in the *North-Carolina Gazette* of March 6, 1778, and later issues as "Just published, and to be sold at the Printing Office, Price Two Dollars and a half, Comprized in Twenty One Sheets in Folio, The Acts of the last Session of Assembly, held at Newbern in December last." Beginning with the advertisement in the issue of April 3, 1778, the price was increased to three dollars.
Weeks no. 43. Evans 15943.
MH-L. Nc-Law (imperfect). *NcU. PHi.*

NORTH CAROLINA. *Laws, statutes, etc.*
The Acts of Assembly of the state of North Carolina. Passed at a General Assembly begun and held at Newbern on the 14th Day of April, in the Year of our Lord 1778, and in the second Year of the Independence of said State: Being the first Session of this Assembly. [Newbern: James Davis, 1778.] [99]
? x ? cm. 20 p.
Title in the above form assumed from caption titles of the Acts of Assembly of other years, as all the copies located lack pp. 1-2 with the title.
Advertised in the *North-Carolina Gazette* of June 26, 1778, and later issues, as "Just published, and to be sold at the Printing Office, Price One Dollar."
Weeks no. 44. Evans 15944.
Nc-Law. NcU. DLC. MH-L. NNB. PHi.

NORTH CAROLINA. *Laws, statutes, etc.*
[An Act for Raising Men, to Complete the Continental Batta-

[89]

lions belonging to this State. April 27, 1778. Newbern, James Davis, 1778.] [100]
Folio. 1 leaf.
Title and collation from Weeks no. 45 (not located). Evans 15945.

NORTH CAROLINA. *Laws, statutes, etc.*
[*Headband of type ornaments*] | Acts | of | Assembly | of the State of | North Carolina. | [*Rule*] | State of North Carolina. | At a General Assembly, begun and held at Hillsborough on the 8th Day of | August, in the Year of our Lord 1778, and in the Third Year of the Independence of | the said State: Being the Second Session of this Assembly. | [*Rule*] | [Newbern: Printed by James Davis, 1778.] [101]
20.5 x 31.5 cm. 4 p.
Caption title on p. 1; no imprint. Running head between rules at top of page: Laws of North-Carolina. In right margin below running head and above headband: A. D. 1778 (over a brace). Also in right margin, opposite the line "At a General Assembly . . .": Richard | Caswell, | Esq; Gover- | nor.
Headband is the same as that on p. 1 of the Acts of April, 1777.
Weeks no. 47 (collated 38 p.!). Evans 15946 (from Weeks).
NcU (2 copies).

UNITED STATES. *Treaties.*
[Treaty of Friendship and Alliance Concluded between France and the United States. Newbern: Printed by James Davis, 1778.]
[102]
Weeks no. 46, citing the *North-Carolina Gazette* of May 29, 1778, in which it was mentioned as "immediately published here." This is presumptive but not entirely conclusive evidence of its having been printed locally. Evans 16148.

1779

NORTH CAROLINA. *General Assembly. House of Commons.*
[*Headband of type ornaments*] The | Journal | of the | House of Commons. | [*Row of type ornaments*] | State of North-Carolina. | At a General Assembly, begun and held at Smithfield on the

third day of | May, in the year of our Lord 1779, and in the third year of the independence of the | said state: Being the first session of this assembly. | [*Row of type ornaments*]. | [Newbern: James Davis, 1779.] [103]
15.5 x 19.5 cm. 33 p.
Caption title; no imprint.
The session lasted to May 15, 1779.
DLC.

NORTH CAROLINA. *Laws, statutes, etc.*
[*Headband of type ornaments*] | Acts | of | Assembly | of the State of | North-Carolina. | [*Line of type ornaments*] | State of North-Carolina. | At a General Assembly begun | and held at Newbern on the 14th Day of April, in the Year of our | Lord 1778, and from thence continued by Adjournments and Pro- | rogations to the 19th Day of January, at Halifax, in the Year of | our Lord 1779, being the third Session of this Assembly. | [*Rule*] | [Newbern: Printed by James Davis, 1779.] [104]
18.5 x 30 cm. 38 p.
Caption title; no imprint. Running head as before. In right margin below running head and above headband: A. D. 1779 (over a brace). In right margin, as before, name of Richard Caswell, Esq; Governor.
Typographic headband entirely different from that of the Acts of April, 1777, and August, 1778.
On p. 38: "Read three times, and ratified in general assembly, the twelfth day of February, anno domini one thousand seven hundred and seventy nine."
Weeks no. 50. Evans 16416.
NcU. NcD (lacking last leaf). Nc-Law.

NORTH CAROLINA. *Laws, statutes, etc.*
[*Headband of type ornaments*] | The | Acts of Assembly | of the State of | North-Carolina. | [*Line of type ornaments*] | State of North-Carolina. | At a General Assembly, begun and held at Smithfield on the third day of May, in | the year of our Lord 1779, and in the third year of the independence of the said state:

[91]

Being | the first session of this Assembly. | [*Line of type ornaments*] | [Newbern: Printed by James Davis, 1779.] [105]
18 x 31 cm. 4 p.
Caption title; no imprint. Running head omitted on p. 1 but on other pages as before. In right margin, date A. D. 1779 over a brace, as before, but the governor's name does not occur.
On p. 4: "Read three times, and ratified in general assembly, the 10 of May, 1779."
Weeks no. 51.
NcU. NcD. Nc-Law.

NORTH CAROLINA. *Laws, statutes, etc.*
[*Headband of type ornaments*] | Acts of Assembly | of the State of | North Carolina. | [*Rule*] | At a General Assembly, begun and held at Halifax on the eighteenth day of October, in the year | of our Lord one thousand seven hundred and seventy nine, and in the fourth year of the independence of the | said state: Being the second session of this Assembly. | [*Rule*] | [Newbern: Printed by James Davis, 1779.] [106]
20 x 26.5 and 18 x 23.5 cm. 34 p.
Caption title; no imprint. Running head omitted on p. 1, but on other pages as before. In right margin, as before, the date A. D. 1779 over a brace, and the name of Richard Caswell, Esq; Governor.
With page 17 the type measure changes from 38 picas to 32, and the size of the leaf from the larger to the smaller size noted above.
On page 34: "Read three times, and ratified in General Assembly, the tenth day of November, 1779."
Weeks no. 52. Evans 16418.
NcU. NcD. Nc-Law.

1780

NORTH CAROLINA. *Laws, statutes, etc.*
[*Headband of type ornaments*] | Acts of Assembly of the | State of North-Carolina. | [*Rule*] | At a General Assembly, begun and held at Newbern on the seventeenth day of April, in the year | of our Lord one thousand seven hundred and eighty, and in the fourth year of the independence | of the said state: Being the first

session of this Assembly. | [*Rule*] | [Newbern: Printed by James Davis, 1780.] [107]

20.5 x 30 cm. 16 p.

Caption title; no imprint. Running head omitted on p. 1, but on other pages as before. In right margin, as before, the date A. D. 1780 over a brace, and also the name: Abner | Nash, Esq; | Governor.

With page 12 the type measure changes from 36 to 32 picas.

On p. 16: "Read three times, and ratified in general assembly, the tenth day of May, anno dom. 1780."

Weeks no. 53. Evans 16913.

NcU. NcD. Nc-Law.

NORTH CAROLINA. *Laws, statutes, etc.*

[*Headband of type ornaments*] | Acts of Assembly | of the | State of North Carolina. | [*Line of type ornaments*] | At a General Assembly, begun and held at Hillsborough on the fifth day of | September, in the year of our Lord one thousand seven hundred and eighty, and in the fifth year of the independence of the said state: Being the second session of this Assembly. | [*Line of type ornaments*] | [Newbern: Printed by James Davis, 1780.] 18 x 24 cm. 11 p. [108]

Caption title; no imprint. Running head omitted on p. 1, but on other pages as before. In right margin, as before, the date A. D. 1780 over a brace, and also the name Abner Nash, Esq; governor.

On p. 11: "Read three times, and ratified in General Assembly, the thirteenth day of Septr. Anno Dom. 1780."

Weeks no. 54. Evans 16914.

NcU. NcD. Nc-Law.

1781

NORTH CAROLINA. *Laws, statutes, etc.*

[*Headband of type ornaments*] | Acts of Assembly | of the | State of North Carolina. | [*Line of type ornaments*] | At a General Assembly begun and held at Halifax on the eighteenth day of January, | in the year of our Lord one thousand seven hundred and eighty one, and in the fifth year of | the independence of the

said state: Being the third session of this assembly. [109]
19.5 x 28 cm. 16, [4] p.
The leaves of signature E have no page numbers and are 15 x 20.5 cm.
Caption title; no imprint.
Weeks no. 55. Evans 17278.
NcU, Nc-Law (imperfect).

NORTH CAROLINA. *Laws, statutes, etc.*
[*Headband of type ornaments*] | Acts of Assembly | of the | State of North Carolina. | [*Rule*] | At a General Assembly, begun and held in Wake county on the [*blank space*] day of | June, in the year of our Lord one thousand seven hundred and eighty one, and in the sixth | year of the independence of the said state: Being the first session of this assembly. | [*Rule*]. [110]
18.5 x 26 cm. 16, [4] p. Signatures [A]-E, each 2 leaves.
Caption title on p. 1; no imprint. Acts ratified July 14, 1781.
Signature E contains unnumbered pages 15.5 x 20 cm.
On p. 16, under Chap. XII, An Act allowing salaries . . . , is the provision "That the public printer of this state be allowed the sum of two hundred and fifty pounds specie per annum for his public services, exclusive of the prime cost of the paper he may expend in printing the journals of the general assembly and the laws of this state, for which paper he shall be allowed by the state auditors or the general assembly."
Weeks no 56. Evans 17279.
NcU. NcD. Nc-Law (imperfect).

1782

ASHE, SAMUEL.
A Charge given to the Grand-Jury at Wilmington, Nov. 30, 1782, by the Hon. Samuel Ashe Esq; one | of the Judges of the Superior Courts. [111]
38 x 29.5 cm. Broadside. Text in 2 columns.
No imprint.
NcU.

NORTH CAROLINA. *Laws, statutes, etc.*
[*Headband of type ornaments*] | Acts | of | Assembly | of the state of | North Carolina. | [*Rule*] | At a General Assembly,

begun and held at Hillsborough, | on the Thirteenth day of April, in the year of our Lord One | Thousand Seven Hundred and Eighty Two, and in the Sixth | Year of the Independence of the said State: Being the First | Session of this Assembly. | [*Rule*] | [Halifax: Printed by Thomas Davis, 1782.] [112]
18.5 x 29.5 cm. and (beginning with signature K) 17.5 x 23 cm. 56 p.
Caption title on p. 1. Imprint on p. 56: Halifax: Printed by Thomas Davis. Acts ratified May 12, 1782.
On p. 32, under Chap. XIII, An Act for ascertaining the salaries of the governor, secretary and other officers of the state, is the provision "that the public printer be allowed the sum of six hundred pounds specie per annum for his public service, exclusive of the prime cost of paper, for which he shall be allowed by the auditors or general assembly."
Weeks no. 57. Evans 17644.
NcU. NcD. Nc-Law. NcSaM (lacking p. 53-56).

1783

ALLEN, WALTER.
Twenty Pounds | Reward. | Lost on the 17th of October, by the subscriber, on the | road between Newbern and Curtis's ferry, a large black lea- | ther pocket-book, . . . | [*15 lines*] | Walter Allen. | Craven Co. Swifts-creek, Decemb. 10th, 1783. | [*Row of type ornaments*] | Newbern, Printed by R. Keith, of whom may be had the Almanack for the Year of our Lord 1784. [113]
27.5 x 20.5 cm. Broadside.
The lost pocket-book contained a number of certificates for values amounting to over a thousand pounds specie and $15,000 "paper." On the verso of the copy described is an affidavit dated December 4, 1787, to the effect that the loser "hath never received any part of the said Certificates nor any Compensation for them and that he did forward by William Blount sundry Copies of this Advertisement to the seat of the General Assembly in the Spring of the year 1784."
DLC.

NORTH CAROLINA. *General Assembly. House of Commons.*
[*Typographic headband*] | The | Journal | of the | House of Commons. | [*Rule*] | At a General Assembly begun and held at

Hillsborough, on the eighteenth day of April, | in the year of our Lord, one thousand seven hundred and eighty-three, and in the seventh | year of the Independence of the United States of America: Being the first Session of this | Assembly. | [*Rule*] | [Halifax: Printed by Thomas Davis.] | [1783.]   [114]
16.5 x 22 cm. 67 p.
Caption title. Imprint (undated) on p. 67.
The session lasted from April 18 to May 17, 1783.
CSmH.

NORTH CAROLINA. *Laws, statutes, etc.*
[*Typographic headband*] | Acts | of | Assembly | of the State of | North Carolina. | [*Rule*] | At a General Assembly begun and held at Hillsborough, on the eighteenth | day of April, in the year of our Lord, one thousand seven hundred and | eighty three, and in the seventh year of the Independence of the United | States of America: Being the first Session of this Assembly. | [*Rule*] | [Halifax: Thomas Davis, 1783.]   [115]
21.5 x 33.5 cm. 50 p.
Caption title. Imprint at end: Halifax: Printed by Thomas Davis.
Weeks no. 58. Evans 18069.
MH-L (lacking p. 1-2). *Nc-Law* (44 p.). *NcU* (2 copies, 1 lacking p. 45-50). *DLC.*

1784

[HAY, JOHN]
[An Address to the Speakers of both Houses of Assembly, containing observations, moral and political, upon the proceedings of the late Assembly. By Tiberius Gracchus. Newbern: Printed by Robert Keith, 1784.]   [116]
A. M. Hooper, writing to James Iredell, November 23, 1783, said of this address "It is to be served up to the public in a sixpenny pamphlet . . . " Hooper said that the style was dull and in many parts ungrammatical and that it appeared worse from the press than in manuscript. (G. J. McRee, *Life and Correspondence of James Iredell*. II, 75, 89, cited by Weeks 1896, p. 248-9.)
Weeks no. 61. Evans 18523 (not located nor collated; apparently taken from Weeks).

[96]

TWENTY POUNDS REWARD.

LOST on the 17th of October, by the subscriber, on the road between *Newbern* and *Curtis's* ferry, a large black leather *pocket-book*, containing the following certificates, viz. one for three hundred and sixty six pounds thirteen shillings and seven pence specie, issued by Willie Jones and Henry Montfort, Esq's, in the name of Thomas Allen, Lieut. deceased; two for about three hundred and thirty or forty pounds specie, issued by do. to and in the name of Lieut. Walter Allen; three or four for ten pounds four shillings each, issued by Coor and Hawks, in whose names not remembrec; and two, for seven thousand five hundred paper dollars each, one of them by R. Cogdell, the other by *R*obert Lanier; and about forty shillings in paper money; and some papers of but little consequence. Whoever delivers the above articles to the subscriber shall receive the above reward, or in proportion for any part thereof.

All Treasurers, Sheriffs, tax-gatherers and entry-takers are requested to take notice if such certificates are offered, and stop them as the property of the subscriber.

WALTER ALLEN.

Craven Co. *Swifts-creek*, Decemb. 10th, 1783.

NEWBERN, Printed by R. KEITH, of whom may be had the ALMANACK for the Year of our Lord 1784.

NORTH CAROLINA. *General Assembly. House of Commons.*
[*Headband of type ornaments*] | The Journal | of the | House of Commons. | [*Heavy rule*] | At a General Assembly begun and held at Hillsborough, on the nineteenth Day of | April, in the Year of our Lord One Thousand Seven Hundred and Eighty-Four, and | in the Eighth Year of the Independence of the United States of America: Being the | First Session of this Assembly. | [*Heavy rule*] | [Halifax: Thomas Davis, 1784.] [117]
20.5 x 25.5 cm. 71 p.
Caption title. Imprint on p. 71: Halifax: Printed by Thomas Davis, 1784. The session lasted to June 3, 1784.
DLC.

NORTH CAROLINA. *General Assembly. Senate.*
[*Headband of type ornaments*] | The Journal of | the | Senate | [*Heavy rule*] | At a General Assembly begun and held at Hillsborough, on the Nineteenth Day of | April, in the Year of our Lord One Thousand Seven Hundred and Eighty-Four, and | in the Eighth Year of the Independence of the United States of America: Being the | First Session of this Assembly. | [*Heavy rule*] | [Halifax: Thomas Davis, 1784.] [118]
20.5 x 26 cm. 52 p.
Caption title. Imprint on p. 52: Halifax: Printed by Thomas Davis. 1784.
DLC.

NORTH CAROLINA. *Governor (Alexander Martin).*
[State of North Carolina, ss. By his Excellency Alexander Martin, Esq; Governor, Captain-General and Commander in Chief over the State aforesaid. A Proclamation [of the Definitive Treaty of Peace]. [New-Bern: Printed by Robert Keith. 1784.]
Folio. Broadside. [119]
Title from Weeks no. 60 (not located). Evans 18821 (not located; apparently taken from Weeks).

NORTH CAROLINA. *Laws, statutes, etc.*
[*Headband of type ornaments*] | Acts | of | Assembly | of the State of |North-Carolina. | [*Rule*] | At a General Assembly

begun and held at Hillsborough, on the Nineteenth | day of April, in the year of our Lord one Thousand Seven Hundred and | Eighty Four, and in the Eighth Year of the Independence of the said State: | Being the First Session of this Assembly. | [*Rule*] | Halifax: Thomas Davis, 1784.] [120]
20.5 x 26.5 cm. 92, [2] p.
Caption title. Imprint at end: Halifax: Thomas Davis.
Weeks no. 59. Evans 18660.
Nc. NcU. MH-L (88 p. only).

NORTH CAROLINA. *Laws, statutes, etc.*
[*Headband of type ornaments*] | Acts | of | Assembly | of the state of | North-Carolina. | [*Rule*] | At a General Assembly begun and held at Newbern on the Twenty Second of | October, in the Year of our Lord One Thousand Seven Hundred and Eighty- | Four, and in the Ninth Year of the Independence of the said State: Being | the first Session of this Assembly. | [*Rule*] | [Newbern: Printed by Thomas Davis, 1784.] [121]
19 x 25.5 cm. 1 leaf, 64 p.
The leaf preceding the first page contains "the estimate of the civil list ... of 1785 ... published by the public printer with the laws of this session," in accordance with a resolution of the assembly dated November 25, 1784. In this estimate is the item "Public Printer, four hundred pounds."
Caption title on p. 1. Imprint on p. 64: Newbern: Printed by Thomas Davis. Acts ratified November 25, 1784.
Weeks no. 62. Evans 18661.
NcU. Nc-Law.

1786

NORTH CAROLINA. *Comptroller.*
Abstract of the Army Accounts of the North-Carolina Line, set- | tled by the Commissioners at Halifax from the 1st September, 1784, to | the 1st February, 1785; and at Warrenton in the Year 1786 — designating | by whom the claims were receipted for respectively. | [1786?] [122]
18 x 22.5 cm. 224 p.
Caption title; no imprint Signed: J. Craven, Comptroller.
NcU (2 copies, one lacking p. 1-4 and 223-224).

[99]

NORTH CAROLINA. *General Assembly.*
The | Journals | of the | General Assembly | of the | State | of | North Carolina. | [*Thin-thick-thin rule*] | Newbern: Printed by Arnett & Hodge, Printers to the State. | M.DCC.LXXXVI.
21 x 35.5 cm. 1 leaf (title), 44, 52 p. [123]
Contains (with separate caption titles):
The | Journal | of the | Senate. | [*Rule*] | At a General Assembly begun and held at Newbern on the nineteenth day of | November, in the year of our Lord One Thousand Seven Hundred and Eighty-Five, | and in the tenth year of the independence of the said State, it being the first session | of this Assembly. | [*Rule*].
The | Journal | of the | House of Commons. | [*Rule*] | At a General Assembly, begun and held on the nineteenth day of | November, in the year of our Lord One Thousand Seven Hundred and Eighty-Five, | and in the tenth year of the independence of the said State, it being the first session | of this Assembly. | [*Rule*].
Weeks nos. 64-65 (from Sabin). Sabin 55633, 55630. Evans 19869.
DLC.

NORTH CAROLINA. *General Assembly.*
Account of Taxes. | [Newbern: Arnett & Hodge, 1786.] [124]
21 x 35.5 cm. 20 p.
Caption title. Imprint at end, on p. 20: Newbern: Printed by Arnett & Hodge, by Order of the General Assembly | of the State of North-Carolina. Issued as an appendix to the Journals of the General Assembly, session of Nov. 19 — Dec 29, 1785.
Evans 19871.
DLC.

NORTH CAROLINA. *Laws, statutes, etc.*
The | Laws | of the | State | of | North-Carolina, | Passed at Newbern, December, 1785. | [*Thin-thick-thin rule*] | Newbern: Printed by Arnett & Hodge, Printers to the State. | M.DCC.-LXXXVI. [125]
20.5 x 35 cm. [2], 42 p.
Chapter XXVII of the laws of 1785, "An Act for ascertaining the Duties and Salary of the Public Printer," provided "That it shall be the Duty of the Printer for this State, who shall be chosen by the joint Ballot of two

Houses of Assembly, to print the Laws and Journals of the General Assembly, the Governor's Proclamations, such Accounts of the Executive Officers as the General Assembly may order to be printed for public information, and such Bills as they may order to be printed for Consideration, and to print the Titles of such Laws as shall pass during each Session, one Copy for each Member, and the Certificates for the Attendance of the Members. .... That one thousand one hundred and six Copies of the Laws shall be printed on a good Type, one hundred and sixty-two Copies of the Journals of each House of Assembly, and one hundred and sixty-two Copies of the several Proclamations, Accounts or Bills ordered to be published; and that the whole of the Laws and Journals be printed on Paper of the same size . . . That the public Printer shall be allowed the Sum of five hundred Pounds by the Year, in full for performing the public Printing, including the Price of Paper and the whole of his Trouble and Expence in distributing the Acts and Journals as before directed; one Half of which Sum shall be advanced at the first Session of the several General Assemblies, the other Half as soon as he shall have produced to his Excellency the Governor for the Time being, Receipts from the several District Clerks . . . that he has furnished them respectively with a proper Number of the Laws and Journals."

The act provided that the laws and journals "be delivered at the Office of the Clerk of the Supreme Court in the Districts of Edenton, Newbern, Wilmington, Halifax, Hillsborough, Salisbury and Morgan," for distribution to the several counties in the respective districts, in the following quantities:

	Laws	Journals
Edenton	176	28
Newbern	180	28
Halifax	130	22
Wilmington	160	25
Hillsborough	150	19
Salisbury	180	25
Morgan	130	15

Weeks no. 63. Evans 19870.

NcU. Nc-Law. NcSaM. MH-L (with title page in photostat). NNB.

1787

CRAWFORD, DUGALD.
A | Sermon, | Preached before the | Cape-Fear Union Lodge |

of the | Ancient and Honorable Order | of | Free and Accepted Masons, | and | a number of visiting brethren. | Assembled at Fayetteville on December 7, 1786, | Being the Day of St. Jonh [*sic*] the Evangelist. | [*Rule*] | By the Reverend Dugald Crawford, | formerly one of the Chaplains to the Scotch Brigade in the Dutch Service, now Minister at Fayetteville. | [*Rule*] | Fayetteville: | Printed by Hodge & Blanchard. | M,DCC,LXXXVII.
11 x 17 cm. 18 p. [126]
NcU.

The independent | Citizen, | Or, The Majesty of the People asserted against the U-|surpations of the Legislature of North-Carolina, in se-|veral acts of Assembly, passed in the years 1783, 1785, 1786 and 1787. | [*Rule*] | [*5 lines, quotations*] | [*Rule*] | [Newbern: Printed by Francois-Xavier Martin, 1787.] [127]
15.5 x 23.5 cm. 1 leaf, 21 p.
The first and last leaves are really blue paper wrappers; the first is printed on both sides, the last on recto only.
No imprint to show place, printer, or date. The address, to W. R. Davie, is dated July 30, 1787, and was advertised in Martin's *North-Carolina Gazette,* Newbern, August 15, 1787: "Now in the press and will be published next week." Some of the copies located have a MS note on the title: "Printed by Mons. Martin Newbern An apology for the Incorrectness of the Press."
Signed "An Independent Citizen" in a letter on the verso of the first leaf, dated July 30, 1787, dedicating the work to "The Honorable W. R. Davie, Esq; counsellor at law, one of the members of the Federal Convention." The author is not known; Archibald Maclaine has been suggested.
The writer complains of restrictions imposed upon jury trials by the legislature of North Carolina.
Evans 20426.
CSmH. NcAS. NcU. DLC.

MACLAINE, ARCHIBALD.
An | Address | to the | People of North-Carolina, | with the | charges against the judges in the last Assembly, | the protests in both Houses, | And other Papers relative to that Business. |

[*Rule*] | By Archibald MacLaine. | [*Rule*] | [Newbern: Hodge and Blanchard, 1787.] [128]
19 x 33 cm. 16 p.
Caption title. Imprint on p. 16: Newbern: Printed by Hodge and Blanchard.
Issued with the journals of the General Assembly, session of November, 1786.
Evans 20595.
DLC.

NORTH CAROLINA. *General Assembly.*
[The Journals of the General Assembly of the State of North Carolina. Newbern: Hodge & Blanchard, 1787.] [129]
19 x 33 cm. 76, 80, 8, 16, 16 p.
No title page in copy described. Contains, with separate caption titles:
The | Journal | of the | Senate. | [*Rule*] | At a General Assembly begun and held at Fayetteville, on the twentieth day of November, in the year of | our Lord one thousand seven hundred and eighty-six, and of the sovereignty and independence of the | United States of America the eleventh, being the first session of said Assembly. | [*Rule*]. 76 p.
The | Journal | of the | House of Commons. | [*Rule*] | At a General Assembly begun and held at Fayetteville, on the eighteenth day of November, ... | [*Last 2 lines as above*]. 80 p.
[*Thin-thick-thin rule*] | Appendix, No. 1. | Bills published for Consideration, agreeable to resolves of the General Assembly. 8 p.
[*Thin-thick-thin rule*] | Appendix No. II. | State of North-Carolina, in General Assembly, January 5, 1787. | Resolved, That the Public Printer publish with the Journals of the present Session, | the Statement of the Receipts and Expenditures of the Treasury (including the 100,000 £. | emitted by the Act of the last General Assembly) from January, 1784, to the 1st of January | 1787, as reported by the Committee of Finance No. 2. | [*Rule*]. 16 p.
An | Address | to the | People of North-Carolina, | with the | Charges against the Judges in the last Assembly, | The Protests in both Houses, | and other Papers relative to that Business. | [*Rule*] | By Archibald MacLaine. 16 p. (See no. 128).
The session lasted to January 6, 1787.
Evans 20594, 20595.
DLC. WHi (lacking Senate Journal).

[103]

NORTH CAROLINA. *Laws, statutes, etc.*
[*Typographic headband*] | The | Laws | of | North-Carolina. | [*Rule*] | At a General Assembly, begun and held at Fayetteville on the eighteenth day | of November, in the Year of our Lord One Thousand Seven Hundred | and Eighty-six, and in the Eleventh Year of the Independence of the said | State, being the first Session of the said Assembly. | [*Rule*] | [Fayetteville, 1787.]
21 x 35 cm. 55, [1] p. [130]
Caption title. Imprint at end: Fayetteville: Printed by Hodge & Blanchard, Printers to the State.
Weeks no. 66. Evans 20596.
MH-L. NcU. Nc-Law (imperfect). *DLC. M. NNB.*

NORTH CAROLINA. *Laws, statutes, etc.*
State of North-Carolina. | An act for appointing deputies from this state, to a convention proposed to be held in the city of Phila- | delphia in May next, for the purpose of revising the fœderal constitution. | [*28 lines*] | Read three times and ratified in General Assembly, the seventh [*corrected in MS to* sixth] day of January, anno Dom. 1787. | James Coor, S. S. | John B. Ashe, S. C. | North-Carolina. | In General Assembly, January 6, 1787. | Mr. Willis, from the joint balloting for members to attend a meeting proposed to be | held at Philadelphia in May next, for the purpose of revising the fœderal constitution, reported, | That his Excellency Richard Caswell, Esquire, Alexander Martin, William R. Davie, Ri-|chard Dobbs Spaight and Willie Jones, Esquires, were elected for that purpose. | The House taking this report into consideration concurred therewith. | Extract from the journal, | J. Hunt, C. H. C. | J. Haywood, C. S. | [Newbern: Hodge & Blanchard, 1787.] [131]
15.5 x 19 cm. (trimmed). Broadside.
No imprint, but undoubtedly printed by the firm which printed the journals and the laws of this session of the general assembly.
NN.

1788

[*Typographic headband*] | To the | People | of the District of | Edenton. | [*Row of type ornaments*] | No. I. | My Friends and Fellow Countrymen, | ... | [Edenton? 1788.]   [132]
17 x 21 cm. 13 p.
Caption title; no imprint. Signed "A Citizen and Soldier." Contains seven numbers. Dated at end "August 1788."
"The hour fast approacheth when the trumpet of calamity will reach you. After having unequivocally experienced the impotent feebleness of confederate America, an efficient government was offered to you; which with disdainful scorn, a majority in Convention have treacherously rejected..."
NcAS.

[MACLAINE, ARCHIBALD, *and* JAMES IREDELL]
[An Address to the People of North Carolina, by Publicola. Answer to George Mason's objections to the new constitution, recommended by the late convention at Philadelphia, by Marcus. Newbern: Printed by Hodge & Wills, 1788.]   [133]
Maclaine wrote as "Publicola" and Iredell as "Marcus." The *Answer to George Mason* "was the work of James Iredell and is dated January 8, 1788. It was first printed in the *State Gazette* [in the latter part of 1787] in fragments and in the pamphlet form was accompanied by an address to the people by Publicola (Archibald Maclaine). It was republished during the same year with additions by William R. Davie and others." (Weeks 1896, p. 264, no. 68a, and p. 249.) Evans 21041 (not located not collated) evidently refers to the second edition, as it is listed under Davie's name.
This defence of the Constitution, earlier than all but the earliest numbers of the *Federalist,* is reprinted in McRee's *Iredell,* II, 186-215. Ford's *Bibliography of the Constitution,* no. 24, identifies William R. Davie as "Publicola," Iredell as "Marcus," and says Maclaine "apparently contributed as well."
Probably Weeks no. 70.

NORTH CAROLINA. *Constitutional Convention* (1788).
State of North-Carolina. | In Convention, August 1, 1788. | [Hillsborough? Printed by Robert Ferguson? 1788.]   [134]
20 x 31 cm. [4] p.

[105]

Caption title; no imprint, but probably printed at Hillsborough by Robert Ferguson, who printed the journal of this convention.
Contains extracts from the convention journal regarding the Declaration of Rights and proposed amendments to the federal constitution. Copies were sent to the federal congress and to the governors of the several states by direction of the convention.
Weeks no. 69 (not located). Evans 21341 (not located nor collated).
DLC (MS Div.).

NORTH CAROLINA. *Constitutional Convention* (1788).
[*Headband of type ornaments*] | The | Journal | of the | Convention | of | North-Carolina. | [*Line of type ornaments*] | [Hillsborough: Printed by Robert Ferguson, 1788.]   [135]
13.5 x 20 cm. 16 p.
Caption title. Imprint at end: Hillsborough: Printed by Robert Ferguson. "At a Convention begun and held at Hillsborough, on the twenty-first day of July, in the year of our Lord one thousand seven hundred and eighty-eight and of the Independence of the United States of America the thirteenth, in pursuance of a resolution of the last General Assembly, for the purposes of deliberating and determining on the proposed plan of Federal Government, and for fixing the unalterable seat of government of this state." This convention rejected the federal constitution pending action by the federal congress on proposed amendments thereto.
Evans 21337 (not located). Weeks 1896, p. 264, no. 72*a*.
NcU.

NORTH CAROLINA. *Declaration of Rights*.
A Declaration of Rights, made by the Representatives of | the Freemen of the State of North-Carolina. | [Newbern: Hodge and Blanchard, 1788.]   [136]
19 x 29 cm. 4 p.
Followed on p. 2-4 by: The Constitution, or Form of Government, agreed to | and resolved upon by the Representatives of the Freemen of the State of North-|Carolina, elected and chosen for that particular Purpose, in Congress assem-|bled, at Halifax, the Eighteenth Day of December, in the Year of Our Lord One | Thousand Seven Hundred and Seventy-Six.
Caption titles. Imprint on p. 4: [Newbern: H]odge & Blanchard.
Printed for the use of the delegates to the constitutional convention of 1788.
Weeks no. 67. Evans 20593.
NcU (badly mutilated).

NORTH CAROLINA. *General Assembly. House of Commons.*
[*Thin-thick-thin rule*] | The | Journal | of the | House of Commons. | [*Rule*] | State of North-Carolina. | At a General Asembly begun and held at Tarborough, on the nineteenth day of No- | vember, in the year of our Lord one thousand seven hundred and eighty-seven, | and of the sovereignty and independence of the United States of America the | twelfth, being the first session of the said Assembly. | [*Rule*] | [Newbern: Hodge and Wills, 1788?] [137]
19 x 33.5 cm. 56, [8] p.
Caption title. Imprint on p. 56: Newbern: Printed by Hodge and Wills, Printers to the State.
The appendix of eight unnumbered pages has caption title as follows:
A State of the Treasury of North-Carolina for the year 1787 — The Public Treasurer's Account Current, together with a list of the | Balances due from several Sheriffs Within the State for the Years 1784, 1785 and 1786. | [*Rule*] | John Haywood, Public Treasurer, In Account with the State of North-Carolina, Dr. | [*Rule*].
The session lasted to December 22, 1787.
Evans 21338.
DLC. Nc-Law. WHi.

NORTH CAROLINA. *General Assembly. Senate.*
[*Thin-thick-thin rule*] | The | Journal | of the | Senate. | [*Rule*]| State of North-Carolina. | At a General Assembly begun and held at Tarborough, on the nineteenth day of No- | vember, in the year of our Lord one thousand seven hundred and eighty-seven, | and of the sovereignty and independence of the United States of America the | twefth, being the first session of the said Assembly. | [*Rule line*] | [Newbern: Hodge and Wills, 1788?]
19 x 33.5 cm. 51 p. [138]
Caption title. Imprint on p. 51: Newbern: Printed by Hodge and Wills, Printers to the State.
DLC. WHi.

NORTH CAROLINA. *Laws, statutes, etc.*
[*Typographic headband*] | The | Laws | of | North-Carolina. |

[107]

[*Rule*] | At a General Assembly, begun and held at Tarborough on the eighteenth | day of November, in the Year of our Lord One Thousand Seven Hun-|dred and Eighty-seven, and in the Twelfth Year of the Independence of | the said State, being the first Session of said Assembly. | [*Rule*] | [Newbern: Hodge and Wills, 1788?] [139]

21 x 34.5 cm. 30, [2] p.
Caption title. Imprint at end: Newbern: Printed by Hodge & Wills, Printers to the State
Weeks no. 68. Evans 21340.
MH-L. Nc-Law. NcU (imperfect). *DLC. M. NNB.*

1789

BAPTISTS. NORTH CAROLINA. *United Baptist Association.*
Minutes | of the United Baptist Association, | formerly called the | Kehuky Association, | Held at Whitefield's Meeting-House, in Pitt County, North-Carolina, | October, 1789. | [Edenton ? Hodge and Wills ? 1789.] [140]

15.5 x 18 cm. 8 p.
Caption title; no imprint. Possibly printed at Edenton, where the minutes of the same association for 1791 were printed.
Evans 21910 (not located nor collated; following Sabin 37166).
MBC.

[HALLING, SOLOMON?]
[A Discourse, delivered before Saint John's Lodge, No. 2, of Newbern, on the Festival of St. John the Baptist, June 24, 1789. Newbern ? Francois-Xavier Martin ? 1789.] [141]

Noted as advertised in the *State Gazette of North-Carolina,* Edenton, October 15, 1789, and succeeding issues. It seems likely, but it is not certain, that Solomon Halling was the author; see his Masonic address of December, 1789, no. 155, below. It also seems likely that this was printed in Newbern, though advertised for sale in Edenton, and perhaps elsewhere in the State.
Evans 21798 (not located nor collated, but with imprint "Newbern: Printed by Hodge & Wills, 1789.") The imprint assumed by Evans is

wrong, as Hodge & Wills removed their *State Gazette of North-Carolina* from Newbern to Edenton in the summer of 1788. F. X. Martin was the only printer in Newbern at the date of this *Discourse*.

[Low, Samuel]
[The Politician Outwitted. A Comedy — in Five Acts, written in the year 1788. By an American. Edenton? Hodge & Wills? 1789.] [142]
Advertised as "for sale at the Printing Office" in the *State Gazette of North-Carolina* of Oct. 15, 1789, and in succeeding issues over a period of ten months. Although it is not certain that this was printed in Edenton, the active interest of the printers in promoting its sale, as indicated by this persistent advertising, makes it seem likely that this work was of local authorship and manufacture.

Martin, Francois Xavier.
A | Funeral | Oration | On the Most Worshipful and Honorable | Major-General Richard Caswell, | Grand-Master of the Masons of N. Carolina, | delivered in Christ-Church, before | St. John's Lodge, No. 2, of Newbern, | On Sunday, the 29th of November, 5789. | [*Rule*] | [*1 line, quotation*] | [*Rule*] | By Francois Xavier Martin. | [*Triangle of type ornaments*] | Newbern: | Printed at the Expence of the Lodge. | [*Rule*] | 5789. [143]
14 x 21.5 cm. 6 p.
Advertised for sale in the *North-Carolina Chronicle; or, Fayetteville Gazette* of February 10, 1790.
NcD.

North Carolina. *Convention of 1788.*
Proceedings | and | Debates | of the | Convention | of | North-Carolina, | Convened at Hillsborough, on Monday the 21st Day| of July, 1788, for the Purpose of deliberating | and determining on the Constitution recom-|mended by the General Convention at Philadel-|phia, the 17th Day of September, 1787. | To which is prefixed | The Said Constitution. | [*Filet*] | Edenton: | Printed by Hodge & Wills, Printers to the State. | M,DCC,-LXXXIX. [144]
11 x 19.5 cm. 280 p.

One thousand copies printed at the expense of a few Federalists for distribution among the people (Weeks, no. 72).
Advertised ("For Sale, By the Printers hereof, Price 10s") in the *State Gazette of North-Carolina* of June 18, 1789, and from time to time for about a year later.
Weeks no. 72. Evans 22037. Sabin 55667.
NN. NcAS. NcD. NcU. DLC. ICJ. MWA. NIC. PHi. RPJCB. Cotten.

NORTH CAROLINA. *Convention of* 1789.
State of | North-Carolina. | In Convention, November 23, 1789. | Resolved, . . . | [Edenton: Hodge & Wills, 1789.]   [145]
19 x 27 cm. Broadside. Text in 2 columns.
No imprint, but presumably printed by the printers of the convention proceedings.
The resolution, signed in handwriting "Sam. Johnston Pres." enjoins it upon the representatives of North Carolina in the congress at Philadelphia to propose eight amendments to the Constitution of the United States, which the convention at Fayetteville had just ratified.
Evans 22039.
NN.

NORTH CAROLINA. *Convention of* 1789.
[*Headband of type ornaments*] | The | Ratification | of the | Constitution | of the | United States, | By the State of North-Carolina. | [*Rule*] | State of North-Carolina. | In Convention, November 21, 1789. | [Edenton: Hodge & Wills, 1789?]   [146]
10 x 18.5 cm. 27 p.
Caption title; no imprint. Includes (p. [15] - 18) "A declaration of rights made by the representatives of the freemen of the state of North-Carolina," and (p. [19] -27) the North Carolina Constitution of 1776.
NN. NcAS.

NORTH CAROLINA. *Constitutional Convention,* 1789.
[*Line of florid type ornaments*] | Journal | of the | Convention, | of the | State of North-Carolina. | [*Double rule*] | At a Convention begun and held at Fayetteville, on the Third Monday | of November, One Thousand Seven Hundred and Eighty-Nine, agreeable to | the Resolutions of the last General Assembly,

PROCEEDINGS
AND
DEBATES
OF THE
CONVENTION
OF
NORTH-CAROLINA,

Convened at *Hillſborough*, on *Monday* the 21ſt Day of *July*, 1788, for the Purpoſe of deliberating and determining on the CONSTITUTION recommended by the General Convention at *Philadelphia*, the 17th Day of *September*, 1787.

TO WHICH IS PREFIXED
The Said CONSTITUTION.

EDENTON.
PRINTED BY HODGE & WILLS, Printers to the State.
M,DCC,LXXXIX.

bearing Date the Seventeenth of | November, One Thousand Seven Hundred and Eighty-Eight. | [*Double rule*] | [Edenton: Hodge & Wills, 1789?] [147]
17 x 21 cm. 16 p.
Caption title. Imprint on p. 16: Edenton; Printed by Hodge & Wills, Printers to the State.
Weeks no. 81.
NcHiC. NcU.

NORTH CAROLINA. *General Assembly. House of Commons.*
[*Type ornaments*] | Journal | of the | House of Commons. | [*Rule*] | State of North-Carolina. | At a General Assembly begun and held at Fayetteville, on the Third Day of Novem-|ber, in the Year of our Lord One Thousand Seven Hundred and Eighty-Eight, | and in the Thirteenth Year of the Independence of the United States of America, | being the First Session of the said Assembly. | [*Rule*] | [Edenton: Hodge & Wills, 1789?] [148]
22 x 37.5 cm. 56, [12] p.
Caption title. Imprint on p. 56: Edenton: Printed by Hodge & Wills, Printers to the State.
The appendix has the following caption title:
An Account of Monies received in Part of the Taxes of the Year 1787. | [*Rule*] | John Haywood, Public Treasurer, In Account with the state of North- | Carolina. | [*Rule*].
The session lasted to December 6, 1788.
Weeks nos. 73 and 75. Evans 22034, 21336.
CSmH. Nc-Law. DLC. M. WHi. Cotten.

NORTH CAROLINA. *General Assembly. Senate.*
[*Typographic headband*] | Journal | of the | Senate. | [*Rule*] | State of North-Carolina. | At a General Assembly begun and held at Fayetteville, on the Third Day of Novem-|ber in the Year of our Lord One Thousand Seven Hundred and Eighty-Eight, | and in the Thirteenth Year of the Independence of the United States of America, | being the First Session of the Said Assembly. | [*Rule*] | [Edenton: Printed by Hodge & Wills,

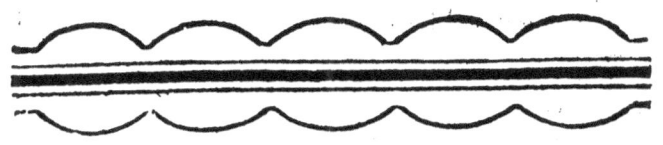

THE RATIFICATION OF THE CONSTITUTION OF THE UNITED STATES,

BY THE STATE OF *NORTH-CAROLINA*.

STATE of NORTH-CAROLINA.

In CONVENTION, November 21, 1789.

WHEREAS the General Convention which met in *Philadelphia*, in pursuance of a recommendation of Congress, did recommend to the Citizens of the United States, a Constitution or Form of Government, in the following words, *viz.*

" WE, the People of the United States, in order to form a more perfect union, establish justice, insure domestic tranquility, provide for the common defence, promote the general welfare, and secure the blessings of liberty

Printers to the State.] | [1789?]   [149]
22 x 36.5 cm. 41 p.
Caption title. Imprint as above (undated) on p. 41.
Weeks no. 74. Evans 22035.
CSmH. Nc-Law. DLC. M. WHi. Cotten.

NORTH CAROLINA. *Laws, statutes, etc.*
[*Typographic headband*] Laws | of | North-Carolina. | [*Rule*] | At a General Assembly, begun and held at Fayetteville, on the third day | of November, in the Year of our Lord One Thousand Seven Hundred | and Eighty-Eight, and in the Thirteenth Year of the Independence of | the said State, being the first Session of the said Assembly. | [*Rule*] | [Edenton: Hodge & Wills, 1789?]
21 x 34.5 cm. 27, [1] p.   [150]
Caption title. Imprint at end: Edenton: Printed by Hodge & Wills, Printers to the State.
Advertised in the *State Gazette of North-Carolina*, Edenton, February 12, 1789, and later issues.
Weeks no. 76. Evans 22036.
MH-L. Nc-Law. NcU (imperfect). *CSmH. DLC. M. NN. NNB.*

NORTH CAROLINA.
[Regulations for the Exercise and Discipline of the Cavalry of the Halifax District. Edenton: Hodge & Wills, 1789]   [151]
Advertised in the *State Gazette of North Carolina*, Edenton, October 15, 1789, and in succeeding issues. There was no established press at Halifax until 1792, though Thomas Davis had done some printing there in 1784. Evans 22038 (not located nor collated, but with imprint "Edenton: Printed and sold by Hodge & Wills, 1789.")

[The North Carolina Almanac, for the Year of our Lord 1790. Fayetteville: Sibley & Howard, 1789?]   [152]
Advertised as "Just Published by the Printers hereof, and for sale at their Office, and most of the stores in town" in the *North-Carolina Chronicle; or, Fayetteville Gazette* of Feb. 1, 1790.
Evans 22179 (not located nor collated).

THAYER, JOHN.
An Account | of the | Conversion | of the Reverend | Mr. John

JOURNAL
Nash. OF THE *Jones*
CONVENTION
OF THE
STATE OF NORTH-CAROLINA.

At a CONVENTION begun and held at *Fayetteville*, on the Third *Monday* of *November*, One Thousand Seven Hundred and Eighty-Nine, agreeable to the Resolutions of the last General Assembly, bearing Date the Seventeenth of *November*, One Thousand Seven Hundred and Eighty-Eight.

THE returning officers for the several counties and borough towns, certified that the following persons were duly elected to represent the same in Convention, to wit, For
Anson county—The Hon. Samuel Spencer, Esq. Jesse Gilbert, Pleasant May, Thomas Wade, David Jameson.
Beaufort—John G. Blount, William Brown, Richard Grist, Alderson Ellison, Silas W. Arnett.
Bertie—John Johnston, Francis Pugh, William Johnston Dawson, David Turner, David Stone.
Brunswick—Benjamin Smith, William E. Lord, William Gause, John Hall, Dennis Hawkins.
Bladen—John Cowan, Duncan Stewart, Thomas Owen, Joseph Gaitier, Thomas Brown.
Burke—Charles M'Dowell, Joseph M'Dowell, Joseph M'Dowell, jun. William E. Erwin, John Carson.
Craven—John Allen, Richard Nixon, Joseph Leech, Thomas Williams.
Cumberland—John Ingram, John Hay, William B. Grove, James Moore, Robert Adam.
Carteret—John Easton, Malachi Bell, John Fulford, Wallace Styron, John Wallace.
Currituck—William Ferebee, Thomas P. Williams, Samuel Ferebee, Andrew Duke, Spence Hall.
Chowan—Stephen Cabarrus, Charles Johnson, Lemuel Creecy, Edmund Blount.
Camden—Isaac Gregory, Peter Dauge, Enoch Sawyer, Henry Abbott, Charles Grandy.
Caswell—John Wommack, Robert Dickens, John Graves, Robert Payne, Robert Bowman.
Chatham—Robert Edwards, William Vestall, John Thompson, John Ramsay, James Anderson.
Dobbs—
Duplin—James Pearsall, James Gillespie, Robert Dickson, Lavan Watkins, James Kenan.
Davidson—Charles Gerrard, Joel Rice, Robert Ewing, James C. Mountflorence, William Dobbin.
Edgecomb—Etheldred Phillips, Thomas Blount, Jeremiah Hilliard, Etheldred Gray, William Fort.
Franklin—Henry Hill, Thomas Sherrod, Jordan Hill, William Lancaster, William Christmass.

Thayer, | lately a | Protestant minister, | At Boston in North-America, | Who embraced the Roman Catholic Religion at Rome, on the | 25th of May, 1783. | Written by himself. | To which are annexed, | several extracts | from a | letter written to his brother, in answer to some | objections. | Also, | A Letter from a Young Lady lately received by him into the Church, | written after making her first Communion. | [*2 lines, quotation*] | [*Filet*] | The sixth edition. | [*Filet*] | Wilmington, (North-Carolina:) | Reprinted by Bowen & Howard. | [*Short rule*] | M,DCC,LXXXIX. [153]
14 x 22.5 cm. 42 p.
On the title page of the Massachusetts Historical Society copy, below the date, the following lines have been imprinted, evidently as an afterthought: For, and at the Expence of | The Reverend Patrick Cleary.
Letters in the text are dated from various points in Europe in the year 1787. A fifth edition appeared at Baltimore in 1788.
NcAS. MHi (lacking p. 41-42).

1790

CARVER, JONATHAN.
[Travels through the Interior Parts of North-America, in the Years 1766, 1767, and 1768 . . . Fayetteville: Printed by George Roulstone? 1790.] [154]
It is assumed that the above title is referred to in the following notice from *the North-Carolina Chronicle; or, Fayetteville Gazette* of September 27, 1790: "Those gentlemen who had not an opportunity of subscribing for this paper at the commencement of the second volume, so as to obtain the beginning of the history of Carver's Travels, are hereby informed, that they can be furnished with that part of the said history which they may not get in their papers, printed separately; which will obviate any objection anyone may have to subscribing hereafter."
At the date of the above notice George Roulstone was printer of the Fayetteville newspaper for John Sibley & Co. Obviously, only a portion of the Carver work was reprinted in separate form, probably from the types used in printing it in the newspaper.

HALLING, SOLOMON.
[An Oration, delivered before St. John's Lodge, No. 2, of New-

bern, the 27th December, in the year of Masonry, 5789, by Mr. Solomon Halling. Newbern? Francois-Xavier Martin? 1790.] [155]

Noted as advertised in the *North-Carolina Chronicle; or, Fayetteville Gazette* of February 1, 1790. It seems likely, however, that this was printed in Newbern; see note on no. 141, above.

Evans 22550 (not located nor collated, but with imprint "Fayetteville, North-Carolina: Printed by Sibley & Howard").

[The Monitor; or a Poem on Dancing, addressed to the Ladies and Gentlemen of the Fayetteville Assembly. Fayetteville; Sibley & Howard, 1790.] [156]

Advertised in the *North-Carolina Gazette* of April 1, 1790, as "Just published at Fayetteville, and to be sold by the printer hereof" [F. X. Martin, at Newbern.] This title was probably printed by Sibley & Howard, who were at work at Fayetteville at that time.

MOORE, JOHN.

[Zeluco. Various Views of Human Nature, taken from life and manners, foreign and domestic. Edenton: Hodge & Wills, 1790.] [157]

Advertised in the *State Gazette of North-Carolina,* Edenton, July 2, 1790, and succeeding issues: "Just Published, and For Sale, at the Printing-Office, in two volumes duodecimo, handsomely bound and lettered, price only one dollar and a half, although the London edition is sold at 14s sterling . . . " In the advertisement the author is described as "the celebrated Dr. Moore, author of the well known travels through France, Germany and Italy."

The London edition of this work appeared in 1789.

NORTH CAROLINA. *General Assembly. House of Commons.*

[Row of type ornaments] | Journal | of the | House of Commons. | [Rule] | State of North-Carolina. | At a General Assembly, begun and held at Fayetteville, on the Second Day of Novem- | ber, in the Year of our Lord One Thousand Seven Hundred and Eighty-nine, | and in the Fourteenth Year of the Independence of the United States: | Being the First Session of this Assembly. | [Rule] | [Edenton: Hodge & Wills, 1790?] [158]
19 x 33.5 cm. 71, 9 p.

Caption title. Imprint on p. 71: Edenton: Printed by Hodge & Wills, Printers to the State.
The 9-page appendix contains the account of John Haywood, public treasurer.
The session lasted to December 22, 1789.
Weeks no. 79.
DLC. Nc-Law. WHi.

NORTH CAROLINA. *General Assembly. Senate.*
[*Row of type ornaments*] | Journal | of the | Senate. | [*Rule*] | State of North-Carolina. | At a General Assembly, begun and held at Fayetteville, on the Second Day of Novem- | ber, in the Year of our Lord One Thousand Seven Hundred and Eighty- nine, | and in the Fourteenth Year of the Independence of the United States of America: | Being the First Session of this As- sembly. | [*Rule*]. | [Edenton: Hodge & Wills, 1790?]   [159]
19 x 33.5 cm. 52 p.
Caption title; no imprint. The Journal of the House was printed by Hodge & Wills, Edenton.
Weeks no. 78.
DLC. Nc-Law. WHi.

NORTH CAROLINA. *Laws, statutes, etc.*
[*Typographic headband*] | Laws | of | North-Carolina. | [*Dou- ble rule*] | At a General Assembly, begun and held at Fayette- ville, | on the Second Day of November, in the Year of our Lord One Thou-|sand seven Hundred and Eighty-Nine, and in the Fourteenth Year of | the Independence of the said State; | being the first Session of the said | Assembly. | [*Double rule*] | [Eden- ton: Hodge & Wills, 1790?]   [160]
20 x 32 cm. 57, [1] p.
Caption title. Imprint at end: Edenton: Printed by Hodge & Wills, Prin- ters to the State.
Advertised in the *State Gazette of North-Carolina,* Edenton, April 10, 1790, and later issues as "Just published, and to be sold at the Printing- Office..."
Weeks no. 80.
MH-L. Nc-Law (imperfect). DLC. NNB.

[The North-Carolina Almanac, for the Year of our Lord 1791. Fayetteville: Printed by George Roulstone (?) for John Sibley & Co., 1790.] [161]

Advertised in the *North-Carolina Chronicle; or, Fayetteville Gazette* of October 4, 1790, as "Just Published, and for sale at the printing office . . ." In the issue of September 20, it had been announced that the almanac was "now in press, and on the first of October will be published."

George Roulstone was first named as printer of the *North-Carolina Chronicle* in the issue of September 13, 1790. With the issue of October 11 the paper was printed by Roulstone & Howard for John Sibley & Co. It was previously printed by Sibley & [Caleb D.] Howard, whose imprint should perhaps be assumed for this almanac.

Weeks no. 86.

PRESBYTERIAN CHURCH. *Synod of the Carolinas.*
A | Pastoral Letter, | from the | Synod of the Carolinas, | to the | churches under their care. | [*Filet*] | Fayetteville: | Printed by Sibley and Howard. | [*Short rule*] | M.DCC.XC. [162]

10 x 16.5 cm. 44 p.

Signed and dated at end: James Edmunds, Moderator. Poplar-Tent, September 8, 1789.

Advertised in F. X. Martin's *North-Carolina Gazette,* Newbern, April 1, 1790, as "Just Published at Fayetteville and to be sold by the printer thereof . . ."

CSmH. NcU (lacking title page and last leaf).

1791

BAPTISTS. NORTH CAROLINA. *United Baptist Association.*
Minutes | of the United Baptists Association, | formerly called the Kehukee Association, | Holden at Flat-Swamp Meeting-House, Pitt County, North-Carolina, October, 1791. | [Edenton: Hodge & Wills, 1791.] [163]

15.5 x 22 cm. 8 p.

Caption title. Imprint on p. 8: Edenton: Printed by Hodge & Wills.

Evans 23152 and 25683.

RP/CB.

CRAWFORD, DUGALD.
[Searmoin chuaidh a liobhairt aig an Raft-Swamp le D. Crawford, ministeir. Fayetteville. [*Latin quotation*]: Air na Clo-Bhualadh Le Sibley, Howard & Rowlston, MDCCXCI.] [164]
12mo. 50 p.
Contains also (p. 29-50):
Searmoin A chuaidh a liobhart aig an Raft-Swamp air an fhicheada' latha don cheud mhios do'n fhoghmnar, 1790. North Carolina, U. S. Le D. Crauford, Minister. [2 *lines, English quotation*] Fayetteville: Air na Clo-Bhualadh le Sibley, Howard & Rowlston. MDCCXCI.
No copy located. Title from Donald Maclean, *Typographia Scoto-Gadelica*, p. 102-103.

HAMILTON, JOHN.
To the Honorable the Speakers and Members of the General Assembly | of the State of North-Carolina. | The Petition of John Hamilton, Esquire, his Britannic Majesty's Consul for the State | of Virginia, in behalf of himself and of Archibald Hamilton & Co. late mer-|chants of Halifax County, in the State of North-Carolina. | [Newbern, 1791.] [165]
21.5 x 34 cm. 4-page folder printed on the 2 inside pages.
No imprint. Dated at Newbern, December 11, 1791, this petition seeks restitution of property confiscated under North Carolina acts of attainder of 1777, together with interest to date.
See no. 181, below.
NcD.

MARTIN, FRANCOIS XAVIER.
The | Office and Authority | of a | Justice of the Peace, | and of | Sheriffs, Coroners, & c. | according to the Laws | of the | State of North-Carolina. | By Francois-Xavier Martin, Esquire, | Attorney at Law. | [*Filet*] | Happy the Country where Law is not a Science! | [*Filet*] | Newbern: | Francois-Xavier Martin. | [*Short rule*] 1791. [166]
11.5 x 19.5 cm. [4], 6, 307, [5] p.
Advertised in the *State Gazette of North-Carolina*, Edenton, August 20,

1790, as "now in the press," with a note by Martin: "Three years are now elapsed, since I issued my first proposals for printing this work by subscription. A variety of causes have occasioned this delay; the establishment of the federal government has not been the least. However, the work is tolerably advanced, and will be completed in a few months." The book was described as "Collected from different authorities, but chiefly from a work of this kind, published in 1774, by James Davis, Esq." In this advertisement the price was 25s 10d to be paid on subscribing. A few weeks later the *North-Carolina Chronicle; or, Fayetteville Gazette* of September 13, 1790, give notice that subscriptions were being taken at that office for the Martin book at 15s 10d payable on subscribing. The Fayetteville paper of December 6, 1790, carried a notice dated November 20 to the effect that "the book . . . being more than half completed, subscriptions . . . will cease to be received on the first of December next . . . " In the *State Gazette of North-Carolina,* Edenton, April 1, 1791 (advertisement dated March 4) is the notice: "Subscribers to The Office and Authority of a Justice of the Peace, are respectfully informed that the work is out of the press since the 15th ult. [February] and that a number of copies have been sent to New York to be bound. I expect to have them back towards the middle of April . . ." Issues of Martin's *North-Carolina Gazette,* Newbern, for April and May, 1791, are not extant, but the issue of June 4 carried a notice of publication of the book: "This day is published, and for sale at the Printing-Office hereof, (Price thirty shillings) . . ."

Weeks no. 87. Evans 23535.

MH-L. NcD (lacking title page and last leaf). *NcU. CSmH. DLC. MH. MWA* (lacking last leaf). *NN* (lacking title page and 3 following leaves). *RPJCB. Cotten.*

NORTH CAROLINA. *General Assembly. House of Commons.* [*Type ornament*] | Journal | of the | House of Commons. | [*Rule*] | North-Carolina. | At a General Assembly begun and held at Fayetteville, on the first day of November, in the | year of our Lord one thousand seven hundred and ninety, and in the fifteenth year of the | independence of the United States of America: Being the first session of this Assembly. | [*Rule*] | [Edenton: Hodge & Wills, 1791?]   [167]
22 x 26 cm. 91 p.

[121]

Caption title. Imprint on p. 91: Edenton: Printed by Hodge & Wills, Printers to the State.
The session lasted to December 15, 1790.
Weeks no. 84.
DLC. Nc-Law (lacks all after page 88).

NORTH CAROLINA. *General Assembly. Senate.*
Journal | of the | Senate. | [Edenton: Hodge & Wills, 1791 ?]
23 x 27 cm. 60 p. [168]
Caption title. Imprint on p. 60: Edenton: Printed by Hodge & Wills, Printers to the State.
Weeks no. 83. Evans 22740.
DLC (lacking p. 1-4 and 33-44). Nc-Law. NN.

NORTH CAROLINA. *Laws, statutes, etc.*
[*Typographic headband*] | Laws | of | North-Carolina. | [*Double rule*] | At a General Assembly, begun and held at Fayetteville, | on the first day of November, in the Year of our Lord One Thousand | Seven Hundred and Ninety, and in the Fifteenth Year of the Inde-|pendence of the said State: Being the First Session of the said Assembly. | [*Double rule*] | [Edenton: Hodge & Wills, 1791?] [169]
20 x 32 cm. 28 p.
Caption title. Imprint at end: Edenton: Printed by Hodge & Wills, Printers to the State.
Advertised in the *State Gazette of North-Carolina*, Edenton, April 1, 1791.
Weeks no. 85.
MH-L. Nc-Law. NcU. DLC. NNB. PHi.

NORTH CAROLINA. *Laws, statutes, etc.*
Laws | of the | State | of | North-Carolina. | Published according to Act of Assembly, | by James Iredell, | Now One of the Associate Justices of the Supreme Court of the United States. | Edenton: | Printed by Hodge & Wills, | Printers to the State of North-Carolina. | M,DCC,XCI. [170]
19 x 30.5 cm. 4 leaves, 712, xxi, [3] p.

[122]

Proposals for the publication of this work by subscription appeared in the *State Gazette of North-Carolina,* Edenton, September 8, 1788 (perhaps earlier) and for a number of weeks thereafter. The proposals announce that the work "is to be committed to the press immediately, and prosecuted with all possible dispatch," and go on to say: "It being impossible to ascertain the size of the volume, and consequently to fix the price, it is proposed that each subscriber advance the sum of 40*s* at the time of subscribing, to be deducted out of the sum of the book, which will be rated at 12*s* per 100 pages. The Publishers pledge themselves, that none of the copies unsubscribed for, will be offered for sale for less than 25 percent, above those subscribed for." The announcement concludes: "It is useless to expatiate on the general utility, or rather absolute necessity of this work. An undertaking of such magnitude having been thought by the legislature to surpass the ability of any individual they at their last sessions offered a loan of 500 £ under certain conditions, to the Printer who would embark on it; but neither engaged to give any pecuniary stipend, or to purchase such number of copies as would ensure a reimbursement of the necessary expenses—relying that the individual citizens, who have more or less suffered by the want of such a Revisal and Collection, would by an early patronage enable the undertakers to complete it. Hence the necessity of publishing this work by subscription. In this flattering hope, and fully confiding in the patriotism of our fellow citizens, we have contracted with the Commissioner, agreeable to act of Assembly, and now solicit the patronage of the citizens of North-Carolina, and of the curious and liberal minded in the neighboring and other states."

The work was announced as "now in the press" in the *State Gazette of North-Carolina* of October 22, 1790. Of its actual publication no earlier notice has been found than that in the *State Gazette* of March 30, 1792, in which it was announced as "Just published and for sale by the printers hereof, (Price four pounds.)"

An appendix, p. 661-663, contains the laws of North Carolina, 1789, and a second appendix, beginning p. 694, contains the laws of 1790. The first of these was printed from a resetting of type. But the second was printed from the same type as was used for the separate issue of the laws of 1790 (no. 169), pages 697-710 agreeing exactly with the pages of the separate issue except for the signature marks and the page numbers.

A number of the copies here recorded also contain a series of supplements, 1792-1800 (and later), with the acts of subsequent sessions. No attempt has been made to note all locations of copies of these supplements.

Weeks no. 88. And see Weeks 1896, p. 265.

Nc-Law. NcAS (3 copies). NcGW. NcSaM. NcU (3 copies). NcW (defective). CSmH. DLC. ICLaw. ICN. ICU. M (2 copies). MB. MH-L. Mo. NIC. NNB. OC. OCLaw. PHi (Tower). RPJCB. TKL. WHi. Cotten.

[The North-Carolina Almanack, for the year 1792. Newbern: Francois-Xavier Martin, 1791.] [171]
Advertised in the *North-Carolina Gazette* of September 24, 1791: "In the Press, and will be published in a few days . . . " The issue of November 5 announced this almanac as "just published."

A Petition and Remonstrance to the President and Congress of the United States. | [Written by a North-Carolina Planter.] | [North Carolina? 1791?] [172]
35.5 x 52.5 cm. Broadside. Text in four columns.
This "petition," with no indication of source or date, is crudely composed in verse in the "Scottish Dialect" with a glossary of some of the unfamiliar terms at the end. It protests against the federal excise tax on whiskey which was imposed in 1791 and modified in 1792. Congressman Steele of Salisbury is mentioned in the text. The New York Public Library dates this "1791?" See William K. Boyd, *Some Eighteen Century Tracts Concerning North Carolina* (Raleigh, 1927), p. 491-503.
NN.

UNITED STATES. *Inspector-General's Office.*
Regulations | for the | Order and Discipline | of the | Troops | of the | United States. Part I. | Fayetteville: | Re-printed by Howard and Roulstone, for John Sibley | and Co. M DCC XC. | [1791.] [173]
12mo. 72 p.
Title in the above form from Weeks no. 82, who credits a copy to NcU; no copy could be found there in January, 1935.
Proposals for printing by subscription appeared in the *North-Carolina Chronicle; or, Fayetteville Gazette* of October 11, 1790. The same paper of January 3, 1791, contained the following notice: "Those gentlemen who have subscription papers for Baron Steuben's military discipline, are requested to forward them to this office as soon as possible, as the book will soon be completed," Evidently, therefore, the book was not issued in 1790, the date on its title page.
Sabin 91410.

[124]

WINCHESTER, ELHANAN.
[The Face of Moses Unveiled by the Gospel, or, Evangelical Truths Discovered in the Law; in four discourses, being an attempt to shew the design of the observation of days, seasons, times and years, as commanded by God to the Israelites: As also the land of Canaan considered as a figure of the rest that remaineth to the people of God. Newbern? Francis Xavier Martin, 1791.] [174]
Advertised in the *North-Carolina Gazette,* Newbern, June 4, 1791: "This day is published and for sale at the Printing-Office hereof ... (Price two shillings and sixpence.)" An edition of this work was printed in Philadelphia in 1787.

1792

BAPTISTS. NORTH CAROLINA. *United Baptist Association.*
Minutes | of the | United Baptist Association, | formerly called the | Kehukee Association, | Holden at Bear-Creek Meeting-House, Lenoir County, North-Carolina, | October, 1792. | [Halifax: Hodge & Wills, 1792.] [175]
17 x 22 cm. 8 p.
Caption title. Imprint on p. 8: Halifax: Printed by Hodge & Wills.
Evans 25684 (under "Kehukee") and 26292 (under "United"); not located nor collated.
RPJCB.

NORTH CAROLINA. *General Assembly. House of Commons.*
[*Headband of type ornaments*] | Journal | of the | House of Commons. | [*Rule*] | North-Carolina. | At a General Assembly begun and held in the town of Newbern, on the fifth day of | December, in the year of our Lord one thousand seven hundred and ninety-one, | and of the independence of the United States of America the sixteenth: Being the | first session of this Assembly. | [*Rule*] | [Edenton: Hodge & Wills, 1792.] [176]
20 x 32.5 cm. 64, [2] p.
Caption title. Imprint on last page: Edenton, Printed by Hodge & Wills, Printers to the State.
The session lasted to January 20, 1792.

The last two pages (not numbered) contain a list of "Grants" of the General Assembly, paid out of the treasury.
Weeks no. 90.
DLC. Nc-Law.

NORTH CAROLINA. *General Assembly. Senate.*
[*Headband of type ornaments*] | Journal | of the | Senate. | [*Rule*] | North-Carolina. | At a General Assembly begun and held in the town of Newbern, on the fifth day of | December, in the year of our Lord one thousand seven hundred and ninety-one, | and of the independence of the United States of America the sixteenth: Being the | first session of this Assembly. | [*Rule*]. [Edenton: Hodge & Wills, 1792.] [177]
20 x 32.5 cm. 48 p.
Caption title; no imprint. The Journal of the House and the laws of this session were printed by Hodge and Wills, Edenton.
Weeks no. 89 (collates 41 p.).
DLC. Nc-Law.

NORTH CAROLINA. *Laws, statutes, etc.*
[*Typographic headband*] | Laws | of | North-Carolina, | [*Rule*] | At a General Assembly, begun and held at Newbern, on | the fifth day of December, in the Year of our Lord One Thousand | Seven Hundred and Ninety-One, and in the Sixteenth Year of the In-|dependence of the said State: Being the First Session of the said Assem-|bly. | [*Rule*] | Edenton: Hodge & Wills, 1792.] [178]
20 x 32 cm. 32, [2] p.
Caption title. Imprint at end: Edenton: Printed by Hodge & Wills, Printers to the State.
Weeks no. 91.
MH. Nc-Law. NcU (imperfect). *CSmH. NNB. PHi.*

NORTH CAROLINA. *Laws, statutes, etc.*
[*Typographic headband*] | Laws | of | North-Carolina. | [*Double rule*] | At a General Assembly, begun and held at Newbern,

[126]

| on the Fifth Day of December, in the year of our Lord One Thou-|sand Seven Hundred and Ninety-One, and in the Sixteenth Year of | the Independence of the said State: Being the First Session of the | said Assembly. | [*Double rule*] | [Edenton: Hodge & Wills, 1792.] [179]
20 x 32.5 cm. p. 713-732.
Caption title; no imprint. To a considerable extent, this is identical, line for line, with the separate issue of the laws of this session. But private acts are included herein by title only, so that beyond the first occurrence of a private act the type and page arrangement differ.
A supplement to the Iredell Revision of 1791 and in some copies bound and issued with and as a part of that volume. See the notes on that title, no. 170, above.
MH-L. NcGW. NcU (3 copies). DLC. M.

NORTH CAROLINA. *Laws, statutes, etc.*
A | Collection | of the | Statutes | of the Parliament of | England | in force in the State of | North-Carolina. | [*Thick-thin rule*] | Published according to a resolve of the General Assembly | By Francois-Xavier Martin, Esq. | Counsellor at Law. | [*Thin-thick rule*] | Newbern: | From the Editor's Press. | [*Short rule*] | 1792.
18.5 x 21 cm. xxvi, 424, [4] p. [180]
Announced in the *State Gazette of North-Carolina* (Hodge & Wills, Edenton) of April 1, 1791, notice dated "Newbern, March 4, 1791," as "Now in the Press..." No issues of Martin's own *North-Carolina Gazette*, of Newbern, are extant for the early months of 1791, but a similar notice appeared in that paper in thte issue of June 4. The publisher said: "It is well known to all those who possess any degree of information, with regard to the system of laws of this state, that these [English] statutes constitute the principal part of its pœnal laws and no inconsiderable part of the rest of its code. As I make no doubt that many more copies, than those contracted for by the legislature, will be wanted, I have opened a subscription book, at my office only, to receive the names of such gentlemen as may be desirous of becoming subscribers to that work. It is offered to them on the terms on which I have contracted with the legislature, viz.: I. It will be printed in quarto volumes, on demy paper and neatly bound. II. The price will be fifteen shillings for every hundred pages: as no idea can yet be formed of the size and number of volumes... As it is not my intention

to raise a sum by this subscription, I shall not ask any advance money from any gentlemen particularly known to me, or who is a subscriber to my Gazette or my Justice, but to guard against imposition, ten shillings shall be demanded from all other persons ... "

The *Fayetteville Gazette* of October 9, 1792, carried an announcement that this work was "Just published, and for sale, at the Printing Office, Newbern."

Weeks no. 92. Sabin 44870.

MH-L. Nc-Law. NcAS. NcGW. NcSaM. NcU. CSmH. DLC (2 copies). ICLaw. LHi. MWA. NHi. NN. NNB. PHi. PU-L. Andrews. Cotten.

UNITED STATES. *Courts: Circuit Court, District of North Carolina.* [*Type ornament*] | Circuit Court of the United States. | North Carolina District. | [*Double rule*] | Hamiltons versus Eaton. | Declaration. | U. S. Southern Circuit, | No. Carolina District. | Circuit Court, | June Term, 1792. | [Newbern? F. X. Martin? 1792?]   [181]

10.5 x 19.5 cm. 83, [6] p.
Caption title; no imprint.
NN.

1793

GREAT BRITAIN. *Court of King's Bench.*
Cases | Determined in the | Court of King's Bench; | during the | I, II & III Years of Charles I. | Collected by | John Latch, of the Middle Temple, Esquire, | First published, in Norman-French, (1661,) by | Edward Walpoole, of Gray's Inn, Esquire. | [*Double rule*] | Translated into the English Language, | By Francois-Xavier Martin. | [*Double rule*] | Newbern: | From the Translator's Press. | [*Short rule*] | 1793.   [182]

12 x 20 cm. 4 leaves, 275 (i.e., 215), [21] p.

Pagination irregular, following the paging of the 1661 edition inset in the margin of the text. Usually found bound with *Notes on a Few Decisions*, 1797 (nos. 232-233).

Weeks 1896, p. 265-266, no. 98a. Evans 25451.

CSmH. NcAS. NcD. NcU. DLC. MH-L. MWA. NN. NNB. PPB. PU-L. RPJCB. Cotten.

MOORE, JOHN.
[The Christian Religion Tried by the Standard of Truth. Or an Enquiry into Some Points of Religion which seem to be much disputed in the present age, and cause much contention and disaffection among Christian Professors of different Societies. Wherein the doctrine of Predestination or God's Decree is considered and set in its proper light. Also God's free Grace and Man's free Will reconciled; and the inconsistencies and absurdities of the Antinomian and Universalist doctrine shewn. In a series of dialogues between Search-Truth and several others of different opinions. By John Moore, V.D.M. Halifax: Abraham Hodge, 1793.] [183]
Advertised in the *North-Carolina Journal*, Halifax, June 5, 1793, as "Just published, and for sale at the Printing-Office, price — One Quarter of a Dollar." Hodge became sole publisher of the *Journal* in February, 1793.

NORTH CAROLINA. *General Assembly. House of Commons.*
[*Headband of type ornaments*] | Journal | of the | House of Commons. | [*Rule*] | State of North Carolina. | At a General Assembly, begun and held at Newbern, on the fifteenth Day of November, in | the Year of our Lord one thousand seven hundred and ninety-two, and of the Independ-|ence of the United States of America the sixteenth: It being the first Session of this Assem-|bly. | [*Rule*] | [Edenton: Hodge & Wills, 1793.] [184]
20 x 32.5 cm. 63 p.
Caption title. Imprint on p. 63: Edenton: Printed by Hodge & Wills, Printers to the State.
The session lasted to January 1, 1793.
Weeks no. 94.
DLC. Nc-Law.

NORTH CAROLINA. *General Assembly. Senate.*
[*Headband of type ornaments*] | Journal | of the Senate. |[*Rule*] | State of North Carolina. | At a General Assembly, begun and held at Newbern, on the fifteenth Day of November, in | the Year of our Lord one thousand seven hundred and ninety-two,

[129]

and of the Independ-|ence of the United States of America the seventeenth: It being the first Session of this As-|sembly. | [*Rule*] | [Edenton: Hodge & Wills, 1793.] [185]
20 x 32.5 cm. 52 p.
Caption title. Imprint on p. 52: Edenton: Printed by Hodge & Wills, Printers to the State.
Weeks no. 93.
DLC. Nc-Law.

NORTH CAROLINA. *Laws, statutes, etc.*
[*Typographic headband*] | Laws | of | North-Carolina. | [*Rule*] | At a General Assembly, begun and held at Newbern, | on the Fifteenth Day of November, in the Year of our Lord One | Thousand Seven Hundred and Ninety-Two, and in the Seventeenth | Year of the Independence of the said State: Being the First Session of | the said Assembly. | [*Rule*] | [Halifax: Hodge & Wills, 1793.] [186]
21.5 x 35 cm. 42 p.
Caption title. Imprint at end: Halifax: Printed by Hodge & Wills, Printers to the State.
Weeks no. 95. Sabin 55638 (not located nor collated)
MH-L. Nc-Law NcSaM. NcU. DLC. NN. NNB. PHi.

NORTH CAROLINA. *Laws, statutes, etc.*
[*Typographic headband*] | Laws | of | North-Carolina. | [*Rule*] | At a General Assembly, begun and held at Newbern, | on the Fifteenth Day of November, in the Year of our Lord One | Thousand Seven Hundred and Ninety-Two, and in the Seventeenth | Year of the Independence of the said State: Being the First Session of | the said Assembly. | [*Rule*] | [Halifax: Hodge & Wills, 1793.] [187]
20 x 32.5 cm. 20 p.
Caption title; no imprint, but presumably printed at the same place at about the same time as the separate 42-page issue of the laws of this session, with which this supplement shows typographic similarity. See note on no. 170, above.
A supplement to Iredell's Revision.
MH-L. NcU (3 copies).

PROTESTANT EPISCOPAL CHURCH. NORTH CAROLINA.
[Address of the Tarborough Convention. Edenton ? Printed by Hodge & Wills ? 1793] [188]
"Hypothetical title of a pastoral letter printed as a broadside and sent out to the churches of the state by the Protestant Episcopal convention then in session in Tarborough November 21, 1793. Probably printed by Hodge & Wills, Edenton." (Weeks 1896, p. 266 — with no indication of his source.)

1794

BAPTISTS. NORTH CAROLINA. *Neuse Baptist Association.*
Minutes of the Neuse Baptist Association. | Holden at Bear-Marsh Meeting-House, Duplin County, North-Carolina, October, 1794 [189]
20 x 27 cm. 4 p.
Caption title; no imprint. Duplin County is about equally distant from Wilmington and from New Bern as possible printing points.
NcWfC.

Hodge's | North-Carolina | Almanack, | for the year of our Lord 1795; | being the third after Bissextile, or Leap Year, | and the 19—20th of American Independence. | Containing | the lunations, rising and setting of the sun | and moon, and seven stars, solar and lunar | eclipses, festivals, remarkable days, &c. | Also, | the militia law, the manual exercise, with | many other useful & entertaining articles. | [*Filet*] | Calculated for the State of North-Carolina, be- | ing adapted to 35 degrees 40 minutes North Latitude, | and 76 degrees 30 minutes longitude West of the | Meridian of London. | [*Double rule*] | By William Thomas, Ast. | [*Double rule*] | Halifax: | Printed and sold by Abraham Hodge. | [1794.] [190]
10.5 x 17.5 cm. [30] p. Title in double-rule border.
Advertised in the *North-Carolina Journal* of Oct. 27, 1794, as "In the press," and in the issues of November 3, 1794, and succeeding dates as "Just Published." The advertisement goes on to say: "A. Hodge flatters himself the workmanship, &c, will be found much superior to any ever published in the state, and the calculations being particularly adapted to

the latitude and longitude of this state, will he trusts, induce his fellow-citizens to give it a preference to any foreign one whatever. The price will be 5*s* a dozen per thousand, 6*s* a dozen per gross, 8*s* per single dozen, and 1*s* single. Paper currency — 10*s* to the dollar. They will be forwarded for sale to most of the postoffices and district towns in the state, and also will be had of the several post-riders."
Evans 27793 (40 p.).
MWA. DLC.

NORTH CAROLINA. *General Assembly. House of Commons.*
Journal | of the | House of Commons. | North Carolina. | At a General Assembly begun and held at Fayetteville on the second Day of | December, in the Year of our Lord one thousand seven hundred and ninety-three, | and of the Independence of the United States of America the eighteenth. It be-|ing the first Session of this Assembly. | [*Rule*] | [Halifax: Hodge & Wills. 1794.]
22 x 37 cm. 67 p.   [191]
Caption title. Imprint on p. 67: Halifax: Printed by Hodge & Wills.
The session lasted to January 11, 1794.
Weeks no. 97.
NcSaM. Nc-Law (lacks the page with caption title).

NORTH CAROLINA. *General Assembly. House of Commons.*
[*Headband of type ornaments*] | Journal | of the | House of Commons. | [*Rule*] | State of North-Carolina. | In the House of Commons. | *Rule*] | At a General Assembly, begun and held at Newbern, on Monday the seventh day of July, in the year of our Lord | one thousand seven hundred and ninety four, and of the Independence of the United States of America the nine-|teenth: It being the second session of this Assembly. | [*Rule*] | [Newbern: Francois-Xavier Martin, 1794]   [192]
22 x 27.5 cm. 11, [1] p.
Caption title. Imprint on p. [12]: Newbern: From the Press of Francois Xavier Martin.
The session lasted to July 19, 1794.
DLC. Nc-Law.

[132]

NORTH CAROLINA. *General Assembly. Senate.*
Journal | of the | Senate. | North-Carolina. | At a General Assembly begun and held at Fayetteville, on the second day of | December, in the year of our Lord one thousand seven hundred and ninety-three, | and of the Independence of the United States of America the eighteenth: It be-|ing the first Session of this Assembly. | [*Rule*] | [Halifax: Hodge & Wills, 1794.]   [193]
22 x 37 cm. 49 p.
Caption title; imprint on p. 49: Halifax: Printed by Hodge & Wills.
Weeks no. 96.
NcSaM. Nc-Law (only 44 p. present).

NORTH CAROLINA. *General Assembly. Senate.*
[*Headband of type ornaments*] | Journal of the Senate. | [*Rule*] | State of North-Carolina. | At a General Assembly, begun and held at Newbern, on Monday the seventh day of July, in the year of our Lord | one thousand seven hundred and ninety four, and of the Independence of the United States of America the nine-| teenth: It being the second session of this Assembly, convened in consequence of a proclamation from his excellen-|cy the governor. | [*Rule*] | [Newbern: Francois Xavier Martin, 1794.]
22 x 27.5 cm. 10 p.   [194]
Caption title. Imprint on p.10: Newbern: From the Press of Francois Xavier Martin.
DLC. Nc-Law.

NORTH CAROLINA. *Laws, statutes, etc.*
[*Typographic headband*] | Laws | of | North-Carolina. | [*Rule*] | At a General Assembly, begun and held at Fayetteville, on the | Second Day of December, in the Year of our Lord One Thousand Seven | Hundred and Ninety-Three, and in the Eighteenth Year of the Independence | of the said State: Being the First Session of the said Assembly. | [*Rule*] | [Edenton: Hodge & Wills, 1794.]   [195]
21 x 33.5 cm. 34, [1] p.

[133]

Caption title. Imprint at end: Edenton: Printed by Hodge & Wills, Printers to the State.
Weeks no. 98.
MH-L. Nc-Law (imperfect).NcSaM. NcU (imperfect). DLC. M. NN. NNB. PHi.

NORTH CAROLINA. *Laws, statutes, etc.*
[*Typographic headband*] | Laws | of | North-Carolina. | [*Rule*] | At a General Assembly, begun and held at Fayetteville, on the | Second Day of December, in the Year of our Lord One Thousand Seven | Hundred and Ninety-Three, and in the Eighteenth Year of the Independence | of the said State: Being the First Session of the said Assembly. | [*Rule*] [Edenton: Hodge & Wills, 1794.] [196]
20 x 32.5 cm. 23 p.
Caption title; no imprint.
A supplement to Iredell's Revision.
MH-L.

NORTH CAROLINA. *Laws, statutes, etc.*
[*Typographic headband*] | Laws | of | North-Carolina. | [*Rule*] | At a General Assembly, begun and held at Newbern, on the | seventh day of July, in the Year of our Lord One Thousand Seven | Hundred and Ninety-Four, and in the Nineteenth Year of the Inde-|pendence of the said State: Being the Second Session of the said As-|sembly. | [*Rule*] | [Newbern: Francois-Xavier Martin, 1794.] [197]
21 x 33.5 cm. 9, [1] p.
Caption title. Imprint at end: Newbern: From the Press of Francois X. Martin.
Weeks 1896, p. 266, no. 101 *a*.
MH-L. CSmH. DLC. M. NN. NNB. PHi. RPL.

NORTH CAROLINA. *Laws, statutes, etc.*
[*Typographic headband*] | Laws of | North-Carolina. | [*Rule*] | At a General Assembly, begun and held at Newbern, on the

seventh day of | July, in the year of our Lord one thousand seven hundred and ninety-four, and in | the nineteenth year of the Independence of the said State: Being the second Ses-|sion of the said Assembly. | [*Rule*] [198]
20 x 32.5 cm. 8 p.
Caption title; no imprint.
A supplement to Iredell's Revision.
MH-L.

NORTH CAROLINA. *Laws, statutes, etc.*
A | Collection | of the | Private Acts | of the | General Assembly | of the | State of North-Carolina, | from the year 1715, to the year 1790, inclusive, | now in force and use. | [*Type ornament*] | Newbern: | Francois-Xavier Martin. | [*Short rule*] | 1794. [199]
20.5 x 26 cm. [vi], 249, [5] p., 1 blank leaf.
Weeks no. 99.
MH-L. Nc-Law. NcAS. NcD. NcU. CSmH. DLC. ICLaw. NHi. NN. NNB. OCLaw. RPJCB. Cotten.

UNITED STATES. *Inspector-General's Office*
Regulations | for the | Order and Discipline | of the | Troops | of the | United States. To which is added: | Rules and Articles for the better Govern-|ment of the Troops, raised, or to be raised, and | kept in pay, by and at the Expence of the United | States of America. | [*Double rule*] | [Edenton ?] Printed and published agreeable to an Act of Assembly | of the State of North-Carolina, | By Hodge & Wills, Printers to the State. | [1794.]
9.5 x 16.5 cm. [4], 73, [5], 62 p., viii pl. [200]
As "printers to the state" Hodge & Wills used either the office of Hodge at Halifax or that of Wills at Edenton. A late advertisement in the *State Gazette of North-Carolina*, Edenton, April 30, 1795 ("Just published, and for sale at the Printing-Office, Price Three Quarters of a dollar . . . ") makes the latter point seems likely as the place where this was printed.
Weeks nos. 100, 101 (not located).
NcU. DLC. Cotten.

WILLIAMS, BENJAMIN.
Newbern, October 6th, 1794. | Dear Sir, | I find that the people,

in the district I have the honor to repre-|sent, are much displeased at the disproportion, between the pay of | the militia officers and that of the private. In some counties, I am told, this | cause of uneasiness is charged to me. | [*26 lines*] | your most obedient and | very humble servant, | Ben Williams. | [Newbern, 1794.]   [201]
19.5 x 23 cm. Broadside.
Mr. Williams explains that the act organizing the militia and fixing the pay of officers and privates was passed before he became a member of Congress.
PHi.

1795

BAPTISTS. NORTH CAROLINA. *Neuse Baptist Association.*
[Minutes of the Neuse Baptist Association. Held at Little-Contentney, Glasgow County, October, 1795. Newbern: Printed by F. X. Martin, 1795.]   [202]
Advertised in the *North-Carolina Gazette* of January 2, 1796, as "Just published and for sale at the Printing Office." It was undoubtedly printed in 1795.

HALL, JAMES, JR.
A | Sermon, | Preached at Suga-Creek, | on | Thursday, February 21, 1792; | At the Ordination of Mr. Samuel Caldwell, as | Pastor of Suga-Creek and Hopewell Churches; | together with the Charge to the Minister, and | the Exhortation to the People. | [*Filet*] | By James Hall, Jun. A.M. | [*Double rule*] [*3 lines, quotation*] | [*Double rule*] | Halifax: | Printed by Abraham Hodge, | M,DCC,XCV.   [203]
12 x 19.5 cm. 43 p.
PPPrHi. NcC.

Hodge's | North-Carolina | Almanack, | For the Year of our Lord 1796; | Being Bissextile, or Leap-Year, | And the 20th-21st of American Independence. | Containing | The Lunations, Rising and Setting of the Sun, | Moon and Seven Stars, Solar and Lunar | Eclipses, Remarkable Days, | Festivals, &c. &c. | Also, | A variety of useful and amusing Articles. | [*Filet*] | Calculated

[136]

for the State of North-Carolina, being | adapted to 35 degrees 40 minutes North Latitude, and | to the Meridian of the central Parts of the State. | [*Filet*] | By William Thomas, Ast. | [*Rule*] | | Halifax: | Printed and sold by Abraham Hodge | [1795.] [204] 10.2 x 16 cm. [48] p.
Advertised in the *North-Carolina Journal*, Halifax, August 17, 1795, as "Just published and to be sold at this office."
Weeks 1896, p. 266, no. 109a (not located).
CSmH. NcU. DLC. MWA.

McCorkle, Samuel Eusebius.
A | Charity Sermon. | [*Filet*] | First delivered in | Salisbury, July 28; | And afterwards in other Places in Rowan, and the | counties adjoining; | Particularly at Sugar's Creek, in Mecklenburg | County, at the Opening of the Synod of the | Carolinas, October 2: | And last, at the Meeting of the Hon. the General | Assembly of North-Carolina in Fayette-|ville, December, 1793. | [*Filet*] | By the Rev. Samuel E. M'Corkle, D.D. | Pastor of the Church at Thyatira and | Salisbury in Rowan County, | North Carolina. | [*Filet*] | Halifax: | Printed by Abraham Hodge. | [*Short thick-thin rule*] | M,DCC,XCV. [205]
10.5 x 17 cm. 64 p.
Advertised in the *North-Carolina Journal*, Halifax, March 23, 1795, and for several months thereafter, as "Just published, and for sale by the printer hereof, (Price one quarter of a dollar) . . . "
Cotten. NcD. NcU. NjP-T. PPPrHi.

McCorkle, Samuel Eusebius.
A | Sermon, | on the | Comparative Happiness and Duty | of the | United States of America, | Contrasted with other Nations, particularly the | Israelites. | Delivered in Salisbury, on Wednesday, Fe-|bruary 18th; and at Thyatira, on Thurs-|day, February 19th, 1795: Being the Day of | General Thanksgiving and Prayer, appoint-|ed by the President of the United States. | Published by the Request of the Hearers. | By the Rev. Samuel E. McCorkle, D.D. | Pastor of the Church at Thyatira and Salisbury, in |

Rowan County, North-Carolina. | Halifax: | Printed by Abraham Hodge. | M,DCC,XCV. [206]
10.5 x 17 cm. 43 p.
Proposals for printing by subscription, dated Halifax, June 6, appeared in the *North-Carolina Gazette*, Newbern, June 20, 1795. Advertised in the *North-Carolina Journal*, Halifax, August 3, 1795, as "Just published and for sale by A. Hodge, Price a quarter of a dollar ... "
Weeks no. 109 (from Sabin 43096).
MBAt. DLC. PPPrHi.

MOORE, JOHN.
[The Doctrine of Predestination, or what is commonly called Calvinism, fairly stated. Wherein many of the most popular arguments and objections used in defence of it, are considered and answered; and the contradictions and absurdities of them shewn. By John Moore, V.D.M. Halifax: Abraham Hodge, 1795.] [207]
Advertised in the *North-Carolina Journal* of Aug. 3, 1795, as "also just published and for sale as above [by A. Hodge], price a quarter of a dollar."
Evans 29096 (not located).

NORTH CAROLINA. *General Assembly. House of Commons.*
[*Type ornament*] | Journal | of the | House of Commons. | [*Rule*] | State of North-Carolina. | At a General Assembly, begun and held in the City of Raleigh, on the Thirtieth Day of | December, in the Year of our Lord one thousand seven hundred and ninety-four, and of | American Independence the nineteenth: Being the first Session of this Assembly. | [*Rule*] | [Edenton: Hodge & Wills, 1795.] [208]
20 x 32.5 cm. 60 p.
Caption title. Imprint on p. 60: Edenton: Printed by Hodge & Wills, Printers to the State. The session lasted to February 7, 1795. Weeks no. 103.
DLC. Nc-Law.

NORTH CAROLINA. *General Assembly. Senate.*
[*Type ornament*] | Journal | of the | Senate. | [*Rule*] | State of North-Carolina. | At a General Assembly, begun and held in the City of Raleigh, on the Thirtieth Day of | December, in the

Year of our Lord one thousand seven hundred and ninety-four, and of | American Independence the nineteenth: Being the first Session of this Assembly. | [*Rule*] | Edenton: Hodge & Wills, 1795.] [209]
20 x 32.5 cm. 48 p.
Caption title. Imprint on p. 48: Edenton: Printed by Hodge & Wills, Printers to the State. Weeks no. 102.
DLC. Nc-Law. NcD.

NORTH CAROLINA. *Laws, statutes, etc.*
[*Typographic headband*] | Laws | of | North-Carolina. | [*Double rule*] | At a General Assembly, begun and held at the City of | Raleigh, on the thirtieth Day of December, in the Year of our | Lord One thousand seven hundred and ninety-four, and in the Nine-|teenth Year of the Independence of the said State: Being the First | Session of the said Assembly. | [*Double rule*] | [Halifax: Hodge & Wills, 1795.] [210]
21 x 33.5 cm. 39, [1] p.
Caption title. Imprint at end: Halifax: Printed by Hodge & Wills.
NcSaM reports a copy with the above caption title, but containing only 32 pages, with imprint on p. 32: Edenton: Printed by Hodge & Wills, Printers to the State.
Weeks no. 104.
MH-L. Nc-Law. NcSaM. NcU. CSmH. DLC. M. NNB. PHi.

NORTH CAROLINA. *Laws, statutes, etc.*
[*Typographic headband*] | Laws | of | North-Carolina. | [*Thick-thin rule*] | At a General Assembly, begun and held at the City of | Raleigh, on the thirtieth Day of December, in the Year of our | Lord One Thousand seven hundred and ninety-four, and in the Nine-|teenth Year of the Independence of the said State: Being the First | Session of the said Assembly. | [*Thin-thick rule*] | Halifax: Hodge & Wills, 1795.] [211]
20 x 32.5 cm. 20 p.
Caption title; no imprint. A supplement to Iredell's Revision.
MH-L.

NORTH CAROLINA. *Laws, statutes, etc.*
An Act to authorize the Secretary to issue Grants for Military Lands, in the manner therein described; and to direct the Secretary | and Comptroller to issue warrants in certain cases therein mentioned. | [Halifax ? Hodge & Wills ? 1795 ?]   [212]
24.5 x 41.5 cm. Broadside.
No imprint and no date; issued about 1795 according to Duke University Library.
NcD.

NORTH CAROLINA. *Laws, statutes, etc.*
The | Acts | of the | General Assembly | of the | State of North-Carolina, | Passed during the Sessions Held in the Years 1791, 1792, 1793, and 1794. | [*Ornamental design*] | Newbern: | Francois X. Martin. | [*Rule*] | 1795.   [213]
20 x 25 cm. [4], 181, [9] p.
Advertised in the *North-Carolina Gazette,* Newbern, July 4, 1795: "This day is published and for sale at the Printing Office hereof ..."
Weeks no. 108 (from Sabin 55583).
DLC. NcAS. NcD. NcU. NcW. MH-L. MWA. NHi. RPL. Cotten.

[PRICE, JONATHAN]
[A Description of Occacock Inlet, and of its coast, islands, shoals, and anchorages, with the courses and distances, to and from the most remarkable places, and directions to sail over the bar and through the channels. Newbern: Francois-Xavier Martin, 1795.]
                                                                  [214]
Advertised in the *North-Carolina Gazette* of December 26, 1795, quoting the copyright entry dated December 12, 1795. Also in the same paper, February 27, 1796, and succeeding issues: "A few copies ... may be had at the Printing-Office, and of Mr. William Johnston, price 50 cents."
"Occacock" probably refers to Ocrakoke Inlet, an entrance from the ocean to Pamlico Sound and thence by the Neuse River to Newbern.
Evans 29351 (not located) from copyright entry in the names of Jonathan Price, William Johnston, and Francois Xavier Martin, as proprietors, for a map and pamphlet.

1796

BAPTISTS. NORTH CAROLINA. *Kehukee Baptist Association.*
Minutes | of the | Kehukee Baptist Association, | Holden at Parker's Meeting-House, on Meherrin, Hertford County, North-|Carolina, September, 1796. | [Halifax: Abraham Hodge, 1796.]
16 x 20 cm. 8 p. [215]
Caption title. Imprint on p. 8: Halifax: Printed by Abraham Hodge.
RPJCB.

Hodge's | North-Carolina | Almanack, | For the Year of our Lord 1797; | Being the first after Bissextile or Leap-Year, | And the 21st-22d of American Independence. | Containing | The Lunations, Rising and Setting of the Sun, | Moon and Seven Stars, Solar and Lunar | Eclipses, Remarkable Days, | Festivals, &c. &c. | Also, | A variety of useful and amusing articles. | [*Filet*] | Calculated for the State of North-Carolina, being | precisely adapted to the Meridian and Latitude of the | City of Raleigh, but will serve without sensible | error for any of the states adjacent. | [*Rule*] | By William Thomas, Ast. | [*Rule*] | Halifax: | Printed and Sold by Abraham Hodge. | [1796.] [216]
10 x 17.5 cm. 48 p.
Advertised in the *North-Carolina Journal,* Halifax, October 3, 1796: "This day is published . . . "
DLC. MWA. Cotten.

[? MARTIN, FRANCOIS-XAVIER]
[A Chart of the Law of Inheritance, of the State of North-Carolina, Exhibiting an Historical View of it, as it stood at the First Settlement of the Country, the changes it has undergone, and its Present State. Newbern: F. X. Martin, 1796.] [217]
Title from Evans 30742 (not located).
Advertised in the *North-Carolina Gazette* of July 9, 1796, as "Just Printed, and for sale at the Printing-Office, (Newbern) . . . (Price 5s)"

[? MARTIN, FRANCOIS-XAVIER]
[A Treatise on the Jurisdiction of Justices of the Peace, in Civil

Suits according to the Laws of the State of North Carolina.
Newbern: F. X. Martin, 1796.] [218]
Advertised in the *North-Carolina Gazette* of May 28, 1796: "This day is published and for sale at the Printing-Office, (Newbern) ... "
It seems quite probable that this treatise was written as well as published by the well-known lawyer-printer of Newbern.
Weeks no. 113 (not located nor collated). Evans 30744.

NORTH CAROLINA. *Courts*
[A Report of a Case lately decided in Fayetteville Superior Court of Law, wherein the following questions are discussed and settled: viz. I. Whether, in the case of a sealed instrument, unattested by any subscribing witness, the handwriting of the party may be admitted in evidence? II. Whether an action of Debt lies upon such an instrument? Newbern: Francois X. Martin, 1796.] [219]
Advertised in the *North-Carolina Gazette* of Apr. 6, 1796, as "Just published, and for sale at the Printing-Office, (Newbern)." Also advertised in the *State Gazette of North-Carolina* of May 19, 1796.
Evans 30743.

NORTH CAROLINA. *Superior Courts.*
[A Few Cases, determined in the Superior Courts of North-Carolina. Newbern: Francois-Xavier Martin, 1796.] [220]
Advertised in the *North-Carolina Gazette,* Newbern, October 1, 1796: "This day is published, and for sale at the Printing-Office, (Newbern;) price 50 cents ... These cases, twenty-six in number, have been copied from the notes of the most respectable law characters in this state."
Possibly the basis of the *Notes of a Few Decisions* published by Martin at Newbern in 1797; see no. 232, below.

NORTH CAROLINA. *General Assembly. House of Commons.*
[Journal of the House of Commons of the General Assembly of North Carolina, November-December Session, 1795. Edenton: Hodge & Wills. 1796 ?] [221]
18.5 x 31.5 cm. 57 p.
Caption title; no imprint, but udoubtedly printed at Edenton by Hodge

& Wills, Printers to the State, who printed the laws of this session.
The session ended December 9, 1795. The journals of the session, and also the laws (no. 223, below), may possibly have been printed before the end of that year.
Weeks no. 106.
Nc-Law (title page missing).

NORTH CAROLINA. *General Assembly. Senate.*
[Journal of the Senate of the General Assembly of North Carolina, November-December Session, 1795. Edenton: Hodge & Wills, 1796 ?] [222]
18.5 x 31.5 cm. 46 p.
Caption title; no imprint. See note on preceding title.
Weeks no. 105. Evans 30911.
Nc-Law.

NORTH CAROLINA. *Laws, statutes, etc.*
[*Typographic headband*] | Laws | of | North-Carolina. | [*Rule*] | At a General Assembly, begun and held at the City of Ra-|leigh, on the Second Day of November, in the Year of our Lord | one thousand seven hundred and ninety-five, and in the twentieth Year | of American Independence: Being the first Session of the said Assembly. | [*Rule*] | [Edenton: Hodge & Wills, 1796.] [223]
21 x 33.5 cm. 31, [1] p.
Caption title. Imprint at end: Edenton: Printed by Hodge & Wills, Printers to the State.
Weeks no. 107.
MH-L. Nc-Law. NcU. DLC. M. NNB. PHi. RPL.

NORTH CAROLINA. *Laws, statutes, etc.*
[*Typographic headband*] | Laws | of | North-Carolina. | [*Rule*] | At a General Assembly, begun and held at the City of Raleigh, on the Second Day of November, in the Year of our Lord | one thousand seven hundred and ninety-five, and in the twentieth Year | of American Independence: Being the first

Session of the said Assembly. | [*Rule*] | [Edenton: Hodge & Wills, 1796.] [224]
20 x 32.5 cm. 20 p.
Caption title; no imprint.
A supplement to Iredell's revision.
MH-L. NcU.

[The North-Carolina Almanack, for the year of our Lord, 1797; and of American Independence, — xxi-xxii, being the 1st after Leap Year. Calculated for the Meridian of Raleigh, 35 deg. 54 min. North Lat. 3 deg. 36 min. Longitude, West from Philadelphia. Newbern: Francis X. Martin, 1796.] [225]
Advertised in the *North-Carolina Gazette*, Newbern, September 10, 1796: "This day is published, and for sale at the printing-office, ... Price one shilling. Stores will be supplied at the rate of six shillings per dozen, thirty two shillings and six-pence, per half-gross, and three pounds per gross ..."

PATTILLO, HENRY.
A Geographical | Catechism, | To assist those who have neither Maps nor Gazetteers, | to read | newspapers, history, or travels; | With as much of | The Science of Astronomy, and the Doctrine of the Air, | As is judged sufficient for the Farmer, who wishes | to understand something of | The Works of God around him; | And for the studious Youth, who have or have not a prospect of further | prosecuting those Sublime Sciences. | [*Rule*] | By Henry Pattillo, A.M. Granville. | [*Rule*] | [6 *lines, quotations*] | [*Filet*] | Halifax: Printed by Abraham Hodge. | M,DCC-XCVI. [226]
12 x 21.5 cm. 62 p.
Advertised in the *North-Carolina Journal*, Halifax, September 6, 1796, as "Just published and for sale at the printing office ..."
Weeks no. 114. Evans 30963.
NcD. NcU (imperfect).

[A Table for Receiving and Paying Gold at the present standard, according to the act of Congress regulating foreign coins. Passed

the 9th of February, 1793. Calculated for the use of the Bank of
the United States. Newbern: F. X. Martin, 1796.]   [227]
Advertised in the *North-Carolina Gazette* of May 14, 1796, as "Just Published and for sale at the Printing-Office."

UNITED STATES. *Inspector-General's Office.*
[Regulations for the Order and Discipline of the Troops of the
United States ... Edenton: Printed by Henry Wills, 1796.]
Title from Sabin 91442 (based on Evans 31472). Not located.   [228]

1797

FREEMASONS. *North Carolina. Grand Lodge.*
[Circular ... July 19, 1797. Halifax, 1797.]   [229]
4-page folder printed on first page only.
NNFM. PPFM.

Hodge's | North-Carolina | Almanack, | for the Year of our
Lord 1798; | Being the second after Bissextile or Leap-Year, |
and the 22d-23d of American Independence. | Containing |
The Lunations, rising and setting of the Sun, | Moon and Seven
Stars, Solar and Lunar | Eclipses, Remarkable Days | Festivals,
&c. &c. | Also, | a variety of useful and amusing articles. | [*Filet*]
| Calculated for the State of North-Carolina, being precisely
adapted to the Meridian and Latitude of the | City of Raleigh,
but will serve without sensible | error for any of the states adjacent. | [*Rule*] | By William Thomas, Ast. | [*Rule*] | Halifax:
| Printed and Sold by Abraham Hodge. | [1797.]   [230]
10 x 17.5 cm. 48 p.
Advertised in the *North-Carolina Minerva and Fayetteville Advertiser* of
November 4, 1797, as "Just published and for sale at the Printing-Office
at Fayetteville and Halifax ... "
DLC. MWA. Cotten.

MCCORKLE, SAMUEL EUSEBIUS
Four | Discourses | on | The general first principles of Deism |
and Revelation contrasted; delivered in | Salisbury and Thya-

tira, on different days | in April and May, 1797. | [*Rule*] | By the Revd. Samuel E. M'Corkle, D.D. | Pastor of the Church at Thyatira near | Salisbury, Rowan County, | North Carolina. | [*Rule*] | Discourse I | [*Rule*] | Salisbury: | Printed by Francis Coupee, | 1797. [231]
9.5 x 17 cm. 56 p.
Discourse II was printed in 1798; see no. 251, below.
NcU. Cotten (lacking title page).

[Martin, Francois-Xavier]
Notes | of a few | Decisions | in the Superior Courts | of the | State of North-Carolina, | and in the | Circuit Court of the U. States, | for | North-Carolina District. | [*Type ornament*] | Newbern: | Francois-Xavier Martin. | [*Short rule*] | 1797. [232]
11 x 20 cm. [8], 78, 83, [8] p.
Weeks no. 115 (from Sabin 44873).
MH-L. NcAS. M. Cotten.

[Martin, Francois-Xavier]
Notes | of a few | Decisions | in the | Superior Courts | of the | State of North-Carolina, and in the | Circuit Court of the U. States, | for | North-Carolina District. | [*Line of type ornaments*] | To which is added | a Translation of Latch's Cases. | [*Line of type ornaments*] | Newbern: | Francois-Xavier Martin. | 1797. [233]
13 x 21.5 cm. [8], 78, 83, [12], 275 [i. e., 215], [20] p.
Same as the preceding, but with the title page modified to cover the inclusion of the Latch's cases originally issued in 1793. The Latch's cases are also found in copies with the shorter form of the title.
Weeks no. 115. Sabin 44873.
NcAS. NcD. NcU. NN.

North Carolina. *General Assembly. House of Commons.*
[*Headband of type ornaments*] | Journal | of the | House of Commons. | [*Rule*] | State of North-Carolina. | At a General Assembly, begun and held at the City of Raleigh, on Monday,

the Twen-|ty-First Day of November, in the Year of our Lord One Thousand Seven Hundred and | Ninety-Six, and of the Independence of the United States of America the Twenty-First: | Being the First Session of this Assembly. | [*Rule*] | Edenton: Hodge & Wills, 1797.]   [234]
20 x 32.5 cm. 54 p.
Caption title. Imprint on p. 54: Edenton: Printed by Hodge & Wills, Printers to the State.
The session lasted to December 24, 1796.
Weeks no. 111. Evans 32593 (not located).
DLC. Nc-Law.

NORTH CAROLINA. *General Assembly. Senate.*
[*Headband of type ornaments*] | Journal | of the | Senate. | [*Rule*] | State of North-Carolina. | At a General Assembly, begun and held in the City of Raleigh, on the Twenty-First | Day of November, in the Year of our Lord One Thousand Seven Hundred and Ninety-Six, and of American Independence the Twenty-First: It being the First Session of | this Assembly. | [*Rule*] | [Edenton: Hodge & Wills, 1797.]   [235]
20 x 32.5 cm. 47 p.
Caption title. Imprint on p. 47: Edenton: Printed by Hodge & Wills, Printers to the State.
Weeks no. 110. Evans 32594 (not located).
DLC. NcD. Nc-Law.

NORTH CAROLINA. *Laws, statutes, etc.*
[*Typographic headband*] | Laws | of | North-Carolina. | [*Line of type ornaments*] | At a General Assembly, begun and held at the city of Raleigh on | the twenty-first Day of November, in the Year of our Lord One thousand seven | hundred and ninety-six, and in the Twenty-first Year of the Independence of the | said State: being the first Session of the said Assembly. | [*Line of type ornaments*] | [Halifax: Printed by Hodge & Wills, Printers to the State.] | [1797.]   [236]
21.5 x 36.5 cm. 68 p.

Caption title. Imprint as above (undated) on p. 68. Pages 26, 27, 62, and 63 misnumbered 22, 23, 61, and 62.
In the Appendix, p. 57, is a resolution of the General Assembly directing the public printer "to print the Militia Law, passed at Newbern, . . . 1794, and bind it up with the laws of this present session of the General Assembly." The text of the militia law occupies p. 57-60 in this volume. On p. 61 is the text of a law concerning divorce and alimony, preceded by a resolution dated December 24, 1796, ordering it to be printed.
Weeks no. 112.
CSmH. NcSaM. DLC. M. MH-L. NNB. PHi. RPL.

NORTH CAROLINA. *Laws, statutes, etc.*
[*Typographic headband*] | Laws of | North-Carolina. | [*Line of type ornaments*] | At a General Assembly, begun and held at the city of Raleigh on | the Twenty-first Day of November, in the Year of our Lord One thousand seven | hundred and ninety-six, and in the Twenty-first Year of the Independence of the | said State: Being the first Session of the said Assembly. | [*Line of type ornaments*] | [Halifax: Hodge & Wills, 1797]
20 x 32.5 cm. 45 p. [237]
Caption title; no imprint.
A supplement to Iredell's Revision.
MH-L. NcU.

UNITED STATES. *Courts: Circuit Court, District of North Carolina.*
Hamiltons versus Eaton: | [*Thin-thick rule*] | A | Case | respecting British debts, | lately determined in the | Circuit Court of the United States, | For North-Carolina District, | Presided by C. J. Ellsworth. | [*Filet*] | Newbern: | Francois-Xavier Martin. | [*Broken rule*] | 1797. [238]
11.5 x 19.5 cm. Title page and 77 p.
Printed from the same types, without resetting, as were used in the *Notes of a Few Decisions* (no. 232, above), with a title page added, the sheet mark "I" being omitted at the foot of p. 77 and the verso of that page being left blank.
Advertised in the *North-Carolina Gazette,* Newbern, February 4, 1797: "On Monday next, will be published and for sale at this office . . . " The

[148]

issue of February 25 carried the notice: "This day is published and for sale at this office ... "
Sabin 30048. Weeks 1896, p. 266, no. 115a (not located).
DLC. NN (lacking p. 25-32.).

WALLIS, JAMES.
The | Bible Defended; | being an | Investigation | of the | Misrepresentations and Falsehoods | of | Thomas Paine's | Age of Reason, Part the second; | wherein also | The Evidences of Revealed Religion are stated, and the | Authenticity and Divine Authority of the several | Books of the Bible are vindicated. | [*Filet*] | By James Wallis, | Pastor of the church in New-Providence, in Meck- | lenburg County, North-Carolina. | [*Filet*] | [*1 line, quotation*] | [*Double rule*] | Halifax: | Printed by Abraham Hodge. | M,DCC,XVII. [239]
13.5 x 23 cm. 115 p.
PPPrHi.

WATSON, RICHARD.
An | Apology | for the | Bible, | in a | Series of Letters, | Addressed to | Thomas Paine, | Author of a Book, entitled, | The Age of Reason, Part the Second, Being an Investiga-|tion of True and of Fabulous Theology. | By R. Watson, D.D. F.R.S. | Lord Bishop of Landaff [*sic*], and Regius Professor | of Divinity in the University of Cambridge. | Newbern: | Printed by Francois-X. Martin, | for Joseph Shute and Durant Hatch, | 1797. | [Price 50 cents.] [240]
14 x 22 cm. 77 p.
NcU.

1798

ARCHIBALD, ROBERT.
[The Universal Preacher; being an Enquiry into the state of the Moral World. No. 1. By Robert Archibald, V.D.M. & A.M. Halifax; Abraham Hodge, 1798.] [241]

Advertised in the *North-Carolina Journal* of January 29, 1798: "In the press, and speedily will be published and offered for sale in the towns of Newbern, Fayetteville, Raleigh, Hillsborough, Salisbury, Morganton, Warrenton, Williamsborough, &c. also at Guildford, Mecklenburg and Iredell court-houses."

BAPTISTS. *North Carolina. Kehukee Association.*
Minutes | of the | Kehukee Baptist | Association | Holden at Caskie Meeting-House, Bertie County, N. Carolina. | Thursday, September 20, 1798. [242]
16 x 22 cm. 9 p.
Caption title; no imprint. Probably printed at Edenton.
PHi.

A | Concise | System | of | Farriery. | [*Double rule*] | [*Type ornament*] | [*Double rule*] | Newbern. | J. C. Osborn & Co. | [*Short rule*] | 1798. [243]
9.5 x 17.5 cm. Title page, verso blank; [2] p. contents; 186 p.
Advertisement dated September 1, 1798, in Osborn's *Newbern Gazette* of November 24, 1798 (no earlier issues located): "This day published and for sale at the Printing-Office . . . "
MWA.

FREEMASONS. *North Carolina. Grand Lodge.*
Halifax, (N. C.) January 20 A. L. 5798—A.D. 1798. | The Most Worshipful the Grand Lodge of [New York *in* MS] | Right Worshipful and Most Respected Brethren, | By order of our Grand Lodge, it becomes my duty to transmit to you a copy of | the Constitution of our Grand Lodge, and an abstract from the proceedings of our last | grand annual communication, holden in the City of Raleigh. | . . . | [Halifax ? 1798.] [244]
19.5 x 32 cm. 4-page folder printed on first page only.
Signed in MS: Robt. Williams, Grand Sec. Addressed on fourth page: Secretary of the Grand Lodge of New York.
No imprint, but probably printed by Abraham Hodge at Halifax.
NNFM.

FREEMASONS. *North Carolina. Grand Lodge.*
The | Constitution | of the | Grand Lodge | of | North-Carolina.

THE BIBLE DEFENDED;

BEING AN

INVESTIGATION

OF THE

MISREPRESENTATIONS and *FALSEHOODS*

OF

THOMAS PAINE's

AGE OF REASON, PART THE SECOND:

WHEREIN ALSO,

The Evidences of Revealed Religion are stated, and the Authenticity and Divine Authority of the several Books of the Bible are vindicated.

By JAMES WALLIS,

PASTOR OF THE CHURCH IN NEW-PROVIDENCE, IN MECK-LENBURG COUNTY, NORTH-CAROLINA.

Thou shalt not raise a false report. MOSES.

===

HALIFAX:

PRINTED BY ABRAHAM HODGE.

M.DCC.XCVII.

| [*Double rule*] | Halifax: | Printed by Brother A. Hodge. | [*Short rule*] | 1798. [245]
11 x 18 cm. 12 p.
NNFM. PPFM.

FREEMASONS. *North Carolina. Grand Lodge.*
[*2 rows of type ornaments*] | An | Abstract | from the | Proceedings | of the | Grand Lodge | of | North-Carolina. | [Halifax: Printed by Brother A. Hodge, M.DCC.XCVIII.] [246]
13 x 20.5 cm. 16 p.
Caption title. Imprint, as above, at bottom of p. 16.
"Agreeably to a notice of the Most Worshipful Grand Master, the Grand Lodge convened in the City of Raleigh on Thursday, the 30th of November, A. L. 5797, A. D. 1797."
IaCrM. DSC. NNFM. PPFM.

FREEMASONS. *North Carolina. Grand Lodge.*
[*Row of type ornaments*] | An | Abstract of the Proceedings | of the | Grand Lodge | of | North-Carolina, | In the Year A. L. 5798. A.D. 1798. | [Halifax: Printed by Brother A. Hodge.] | [1798.] [247]
12.5 x 20 cm. 24 p.
Caption title. Imprint as above (without date) on p. 24.
NNFM. PPFM.

Hodge's | North-Carolina | Almanack, | For the Year of our Lord 1799; | Being the Third after Bissextile or Leap-Year, | And the 23d-24th of American Independence. | Containing | The Lunations, Rising and Setting of the Sun, | Moon and Seven Stars, Solar and Lunar | Eclipses, Remarkable Days, | Festivals, &c., &c. | Also, | A variety of useful and amusing Articles. | [*Filet*] | Calculated for the State of North-Carolina, being | precisely adapted to the Meridian and Latitude of the | City of Raleigh, but will serve without sensible | error for any of the states adjacent. | [*Rule*] | By William Thomas, Ast. | [*Rule*] | Halifax: | Printed and Sold by Abraham Hodge. | [1798.] [248]
11 x 18 cm. 48 p.

HODGE's
NORTH-CAROLINA
ALMANACK,

For the Year of our LORD 1799;

Being the Third after Biffextile or Leap-Year, And the 23d—24th of AMERICAN INDEPENDENCE.

CONTAINING

The Lunations, Rifing and Setting of the Sun, Moon and Seven Stars, Solar and Lunar Eclipfes, Remarkable Days, Feftivals, &c. &c.

ALSO,

A variety of ufeful and amufing Articles.

Calculated for the State of NORTH-CAROLINA, being precifely adapted to the Meridian and Latitude of the City of RALEIGH, but will ferve without fenfible error for any of the ftates adjacent.

By WILLIAM THOMAS, *Aſt.*

HALIFAX:
PRINTED and SOLD by ABRAHAM HODGE

Advertised in the *North-Carolina Minerva and Fayetteville Advertiser* (Hodge & Boylan) of November 3, 1798, as "Just published and for sale at the Printing-Offices at Fayetteville and Halifax, . . . Price — Forty dollars per thousand, or four cents each; twenty-five dollars per five hundred, or five cents each; five and a half dollars per hundred, or five and a half cents each; three dollars per fifty, or six cents each; and seventy-five cents per dozen."
Cotten. *MWA*.

JOHNSON, THOMAS.
Every Man his own | Doctor; | or the | Poor Man's Family Physician. | Prescribing | Plain, safe, and easy means to cure them-| selves, of the most disorders incident to this | climate; with very little charge, the medicines | being the growth of this country, and about | almost every man's Plantation. | [*Rule*] | By Thomas Johnson. | *Rule* | Salisbury: | Printed for the Author, 1798. [249]
8.5 x 17 cm. v, 50 p.
Cotten. *NcD*.

MCCORKLE, SAMUEL EUSEBIUS.
A | Discourse, | on | The Doctrine and Duty | of keeping the | Sabbath, | [*Filet*] | By Samuel E. McCorkle, D.D. | Pastor of the Church of Thyatira, near | Salisbury, Rowan County, | North-Carolina. | [*Thick-thin rule*] | Salisbury: | Printed by John M. Slump, at | Michael Brown's English and German | Printing-Office. MDCCXCVIII. [250]
11 x 17 cm.
Preface dated "Westfield, near Salisbury, September 14, 1798."
NcU. NjP. Cotten.

MCCORKLE, SAMUEL EUSEBIUS.
Four | Discourses, | on | The general first Principles of Deism and Reve-|lation contrasted; delivered in Salisbury, | and Thyatira, on different days | in April & May, 1797. | [*Filet*] | By the Revd. Samuel E. M'Corkle, D.D. | Pastor of the Church at Thyatira, near Salisbury, | Rowan County, North-Carolina. | [*Rule*]

| Discourse II. | [*Rule*] | Salisbury, | Printed by Francis Coupee, & John M. Slump, | at their English and German Printing-Office. | MDCCXCVIII. [251]
11.5 x 18.5 cm. 1 leaf, [3]-42 p.
Discourse I appeared in 1797 (see no. 231). No record has been found of the third and fourth of this series of discourses.
NcU. NcAS. PPPrHi. Cotten.

McCorkle, Samuel Eusebius.
Three | Discourses | on the terms of | Christian Communion. | In the first of which, certain principles are at-|tempted to be established in order from them | to deduce in the ensuing Discourses | the Doctrines and Precepts that | ought to be made terms. | [*Rule*] | By the Rev. Samuel Eusebius M'Corkle, | D.D. Pastor of the Church at Thyatira, near | Salisbury, Rowan County, (N. C.) | [*Rule*] | Discourse I. | [*Rule*] | [*4 lines, quotation*] | [*Ornamental rule*] | Salisbury: | Printed by Francis Coupee & John M. Slump, | at their English and German Printing Office. | MDCCXCVIII. [252]
11.5 x 18.5 cm. 50 p.
No record has been found of the second and third discourses in this series.
NcU. NcC. Cotten.

McCorkle, Samuel Eusebius.
The | Work of God | for | The French Republic, | and | then her reformation or ruin; | or, | The novel and useful experiment of | National Deism, to us and all | future ages. | [*Rule*] | By Samuel E. M'Corkle D.D. Pastor of the | Church at Thyatira, Rowan County, N. C. | In a Discourse delivered at Thyatira and in Salisbury | on the Fast-Day appointed by the President, | May 9, 1798. | [*Rule*] | Salisbury: | [*Broken rule*] | Printed by Francis Coupee. | M.DCC.XCVIII. [253]
9 x 15.5 cm. 45 p.
DLC. PPPrHi.

NORTH CAROLINA. *General Assembly. House of Commons.*
[*Row of type ornaments*] | Journal | of the | House of Commons. | [*Thick-thin rule*] | State of North Carolina. | At a General Assembly, begun and held in the City of Raleigh, on Monday | the twentieth of November, in the year of our Lord one thousand seven hun-|dred and ninety-seven, and of American Independence the twenty-second; it be-|ing the first session of this Assembly. | [Halifax: Abraham Hodge, 1798.]   [254]
22.5 x 37.5 cm. 56 p.
Caption title. Imprint on p. 56: Halifax: Printed by Abraham Hodge, Printer to the State.
The session lasted to December 23, 1797.
Weeks no. 117.
MiD-B. Nc-Law. CSmH. DLC. M. WHi.

NORTH CAROLINA. *General Assembly. Senate.*
[*Row of type ornaments*] | Journal | of the | Senate. | [*Thick-thin rule*] | State of North Carolina. | At a General Assembly, begun and held in the City of Raleigh, on Monday | the twentieth of November, in the year of our Lord one thousand seven hun-|dred and ninety-seven, and of American Independence the twenty-second; it be-|ing the first session of this Assembly. | [Halifax: Abraham Hodge, 1798.]   [255]
22.3 x 37.3 cm. 44 p.
Caption title. Imprint on p. 44: Halifax: Printed by Abraham Hodge, Printer to the State.
Weeks no. 116.
MiD-B. NcD. Nc-Law (imperfect). CSmH. DLC. M. WHi.

NORTH CAROLINA. *Laws, statutes, etc.*
[*Typographic headband*] | Laws | of | North-Carolina. | [*Rule*] | At a General Assembly begun and held at Raleigh, on the twentieth day of | November, in the year of our Lord one thousand seven hundred and ninety-seven, | in the twenty-second year of the Independence of the said State: Being the first Session

[156]

of the said Assembly. | [*Rule*] | [Halifax: Printed by Abraham Hodge, Printer to the State.] | [1798.] [256]
22 x 37 cm. 25, [1] p.
Caption title. Imprint as above (undated) at end.
Weeks no. 118.
CSmH. DLC. M. MH-L. NNB. PHi. RPL.

NORTH CAROLINA. *Laws, statutes, etc.*
[*Typographic headband*] | Laws | of | North-Carolina. | [*Rule*] | At a General Assembly, begun and held at Raleigh, on the twentieth day of | November, in the year of our Lord one thousand seven hundred and ninety-seven, | in the twenty-second year of the Independence of the said State: Being the first Session of the said Assembly. | [*Rule*] | [Halifax: Abraham Hodge, 1798.] [257]
20 x 32.5 cm. 15 p.
Caption title; no imprint.
A supplement to Iredell's Revision.
MH-L. NcU.

The | North-Carolina | Almanack, | For the Year of our Lord 1799; | Being the third after Bissextile or Leap-Year, | and the 23d-24th of American Independence. | Containing | The Lunations, Rising and Setting of the Sun, Moon | and Seven Stars, Solar and Lunar Eclipses, | Remarkable Days, Festivals, &c. &c. | Also, | A variety of useful and amusing articles. | [*Filet*] | Calculated for the State of North-Carolina, | being precisely adapted to the Meridian and | Latitude of the Town of Salisbury, | but will serve without any sensible error | for any of the states adjacent. | [*Rule*] | Salisbury: | Printed and sold, wholesale and retail, | by Francis Coupee. | [1798.] [258]
10 x 17 cm. [401] p.
Evans 34249.
DLC. Cotten.

[The North-Carolina Almanack, for the year of our Lord, 1799; and of American Independence, 23-24. Being the 3d after Leap Year. Calculated for the Meridian of Newbern, 35 Deg. 4 Min. North Lat. 2 Deg. 61 [?] Min. Long. West from Philadelphia. Newbern: Printed for John C. Osborn & Co. ? 1798.]   [259]
Advertised in the *Newbern Gazette* of November 24, 1798, as "Just published and for sale at this office."
Evans 34248 (not located).

1799

BAPTISTS. *North Carolina. Neuse Baptist Association.*
[*Type ornament*] | Minutes | of the | North-Carolina | Neuse Baptist Association, | holden at Poplar Spring Meeting-House, | Franklin County. | [*Rule*] | Friday, October 18, 1799. | [Raleigh: Joseph Gales, 1799.]   [260]
13 x 20 cm. 8 p.
Caption title. Imprint on p. 8: Printed by J. Gales, Raleigh.
PCA.

DAVIE, WILLIAM RICHARDSON.
Instructions | to be observed for the | formations and movements | of the | Cavalry. | [*Rule*] | [*Long rule*] | Published agreeably to a Resolution of the Legislature of North-Carolina. | [*Long rule*] | By William Richardson Davie, Esquire. | Governor, Captain-General and Commander in Chief of the Militia of the | State of North-Carolina. | [*Double rule*] | Halifax: | Printed by Abraham Hodge. | M.DCC.XCIX.   [261]
12 x 19.5 cm. ix, [2], 180 p., 3 plates.
Advertised in Hodge & Boylan's *North-Carolina Minerva and Raleigh Advertiser* of October 29, 1799, as "Just published and for sale at this office..." The same paper of July 9, 1799, carried a notice dated April 29, 1799, that this work was in the press: "It being supposed that the 150 copies taken by the public are scarcely sufficient to supply the whole of the commissioned officers and that these Instructions would be a desirable acquisition at the present crisis to private gentlemen, an extra number is printed. It will be printed on a good Paper, in a distinct and legible man-

ner, and contain upwards of 180 octavo Pages, with Copperplates illustrating the Manoeuvres, Evolutions, &c. It will be delivered to the subscribers in the towns of Newbern, Edenton, Tarborough, Fayetteville, Salem, Hillsborough, and at the printing office in the town of Halifax, and city of Raleigh, bound in boards, at One Dollar. A. Hodge. N. B. The price to non-subscribers will be One Dollar and a quarter."
Stephen B. Weeks, "Libraries and Literature in North Carolina in the Eighteenth Century," American Historical Association *Annual Report* for 1895, p. 259, mentions two editions of this — "the first in 1798 and the second, revised and enlarged, in 1799 (Halifax)." The above publisher's notice of 1799 says nothing of an earlier edition, but the preface of the 1799 edition says that "The policy of placing our own cavalry on a footing with the cavalry of Europe, rendered several additions necessary to the small work contemplated by the Legislature, which had been published by Col. Davie for the use of his own regiment." See Weeks 1891, no. 119. The New York Public Library copy is from the library of George Washington, with his autograph.
Weeks no. 124. Sabin 18748.
NN. NcAS. NcD. NcWfC. NcU. MoS. NWM. Cotten.

FREEMASONS. *North Carolina. Grand Lodge.*
[*Row of type ornaments*] | An | Abstract of the Proceedings | of the | Grand Lodge | of North-Carolina, | In the Year A.L. 5799. A.D. 1799. | [Raleigh — Printed by Brothers Hodge & Boylan.] | [1799.]   [262]
12.5 x 20 cm. 28 p.
Caption title. Imprint as above (without date) on p. 28.
NNFM. PPFM.

Hodge & Boylan's | North-Carolina | Almanack, | For the Year of our Lord 1800: | Being Bissextile or Leap-Year in course, but | will be counted as a common year. | And the 24th — 25th of American Independence. | [*11 lines*] | [*Rule*] | By William Thomas, Ast. | [*Rule*] | Halifax: | Printed and Sold by Abraham Hodge. | [1799.]   [263]
11 x 18 cm. 48 p.
The lines omitted above are the same as in the title of *Hodge's North-Carolina Almanack* for 1799 (no. 248, above).

[159]

Advertised in the *North-Carolina Minerva and Raleigh Advertiser* of November 26, 1799, as "Just published [by Hodge & Boylan], and for sale at their Printing offices in Halifax and Raleigh, at 40 dollars per 1000, . . . and a shilling a piece . . . "
MWA. Cotten.

MILLER, ROBERT JOHNSTON.
An | Introduction | to the | Knowledge | of the | Christian Religion. | [*Short rule*] | Published for the use of the Protestant Episco-|pal Church of Whitehaven Parish. | [*Rule*] | By Robert Johnston Miller, R. P. | [*Double rule*] | Salisbury; | Printed, by John M. Slump, | at Michael Brown's Printing-Office. | MDCCXCIX. [264]
10 x 16.5 cm. 50 p.
Cotten.

NORTH CAROLINA. *Courts: Superior Courts of Law and Equity.*
Reports | of | Cases Adjudged | in the | Superior Courts of Law and Equity | of the | State of North-Carolina, | from the year 1789, to the year 1798. | [*Rule*] | By John Haywood, Esquire, | one of the judges of the Superior Courts of Law and Equity. | [*Rule*] | Halifax: | Printed by Abraham Hodge. | M,DCC,XCIX.
12 x 20.5 cm. [4], 502, [18] p. [265]
The second volume of Haywood's North Carolina reports was issued in 1806.
Weeks no. 123. Evans 35607.
MWA. NcAS. NcD. DLC. M. MH-L. NN. NNB. OCLaw. RPJCB. Cotten

NORTH CAROLINA. *General Assembly. House of Commons.*
[*Headband of type ornaments*] | Journal | of the | House of Commons. | [*Heavy rule*] | State of North-Carolina. | In the House of Commons. | [*Line of type ornaments*] | At a General Assembly begun and held at the City of Raleigh, on Monday the nine-|teenth day of November, in the year of our Lord one

thousand seven hundred and ninety-eight, | and of the Independence of the United States of America the twenty-third: It being the | First Session of this Assembly. | [*Line of type ornaments*] | [Wilmington: Allmand Hall, 1799.] [266]
28 x 30 cm. 80 p.
Caption title; no imprint. The session lasted to December 24, 1798.
Allmand Hall's *Wilmington Gazette* of April 19, 1799, contained the following notice:
"The Laws & Journals of the last session of the General Assembly . . . will be completed and ready for delivery the latter end of this week, . . . The deprivation of a house and the destruction of a part of my printing apparatus, by the late fire, have in a great measure retarded their publication — these circumstances produced unavoidable obstacles to the speedy execution of business, during the inclemency of the winter, which I hope will be a sufficient apology for their not being ready at a much earlier period. In consequence of a promise to the members of the General Assembly, to establish a Printing-office at the seat of government, previous to the ensuing session, and in obedience to an act entitled "An act more fully to ascertain the duties of the Public Printer," I have made arrangements for that purpose, and am in daily expectation of receiving from New-York, a complete set of printing apparatus, with every other necessary, for the dispatch of business; which, when received will be immediately forwarded to Raleigh, where . . . I intend publishing . . . a Newspaper, to be entitled The Courier, or North-Carolina State Gazette; (notwithstanding the opposition lately manifested by the removal of the Fayetteville Minerva office to that place.)"
In spite of this announcement, Hall did not remove to Raleigh, but continued to publish his *Gazette* at Wilmington.
Weeks no. 121.
DLC. Nc-Law.

NORTH CAROLINA. *General Assembly. Senate.*
[*Headband of type ornaments*] | Journal | of the | Senate. | [*Thick rule*] | State of North-Carolina. | In the Senate. | [*Line of type ornaments*] | At a General Assembly begun and held at the City of Raleigh, on Monday the nine-|teenth day of November, in the year of our Lord one thousand seven hundred and ninety-eight, | and of the Independence of the United States of

America the twenty-third: It being the | First Session of this Assembly. | [*Line of type ornaments*] | [Wilmington: A. Hall, 1799.] [267]
18 x 29.5 cm. 79 p.
Caption title. Imprint on p. 79: Wilmington, (N. C.) Printed by A. Hall, Printer to the State.
Weeks no. 120.
DLC. Nc-Law.

NORTH CAROLINA. *Laws, statutes, etc.*
[*Typographic headband*] | Laws | of | North-Carolina. | [*Line of type ornaments*] | At a General Assembly begun and held at the City of Raleigh, on Monday the | nineteenth day of November, in the year of our Lord one thousand seven hundred and | ninety-eight, and of the Independence of the United States of America the twenty-third: | It being the First Session of this Assembly. | [*Line of type ornaments*] | [Wilmington: A. Hall, 1799.] [268]
21 x 30 cm. 55, [3] p.
Caption title. Imprint at end: Wilmington, (N. C.) Printed by A. Hall, Printer to the State.
Weeks no. 122. Evans 34247.
MH-L. Nc-Law. NcU. CSmH. DLC. M. NN. NNB. PHi.

NORTH CAROLINA. *Laws, statutes, etc.*
[*Typographic headband*] | Laws | of | North-Carolina. | [*Thick-thin rule*] | At a General Assembly, begun and held at the City of Raleigh, | on Monday the nineteenth day of November, in the year of our Lord | one thousand seven hundred and ninety-eight, and of the Independence | of the United States of America the twenty-third: It being the First Session of this Assembly. | [*Thin-thick rule*] | [Wilmington: A. Hall, 1799.] [269]
20 x 32.5 cm. 27 p.
Caption title; no imprint.
A supplement to Iredell's Revision.
MH-L. NcU.

NORTH CAROLINA. *Laws, statutes, etc.*
[The Militia Laws, now in force in the State of North Carolina. Extracted from the several acts of the General Assembly of the State of North-Carolina. And Published according to the resolution of the officers composing the Court Martial of the first battalion of Cavalry, and of the resolution of the officers composing the Court-Martial of the first battalion of infantry, of Rowan Militia. Salisbury: Francis Coupee, 1799.] [270]
Advertised in the *North-Carolina Mercury and Salisbury Advertiser* of June 27, 1799: "This day is published, by Francis Coupee, and for sale at his Printing Office, Salisbury . . . The several Subscribers to the above laws, may receive their copies by applying at this office."

UNITED STATES. *Laws, statutes, etc.*
Supplement to the North-Carolina Journal. No. 357. | Halifax: Printed by A. Hodge. | [*Line of type ornaments*] | Acts | passed at the | Third Session | of the | Fifth Congress | of the | United States. | [*Line of type ornaments*] | [Halifax: Abraham Hodge. 1799.] [271]
22 x 36.5 cm. 123, [1] p.
No. 357 of the *North-Carolina Journal* was dated May 20, 1799.
MH-L.

UNITED STATES. *Treaties.*
[Articles of a Treaty between the United States of America and the Cherokee Indians. Halifax, 1799.] [272]
Not located. Title from Anderson Catalogue 1912, January 1925, no. 365.

1800

ADDISON, ALEXANDER.
Analysis | of | The Report of the Committee | of the | Virginia Assembly, | on the | Proceedings of sundry of the other States | in | Answer to their Resolutions. | [*Rule*] | By Alexander Addison. | [*Rule*] | Raleigh: | Printed by Hodge Boylan. 1800. [273]
10.5 x 19 cm. 54 p.
NN.

[163]

Animadversions on | James Holland's | Strictures | on General | Joseph Dicksons | Circular Letter, | of the first of May 1800. | [*Broken rule*] | Lincolnton: (N. C.) | Printed, by John Martin Slump, at his Printing-Office, | near the Public Square. 1800.
11.5 x 19.5 cm. 15 p. [274]
Signed at end: A True Republican Federalist.
Sabin 32506.
NcU.

CALDWELL, JOSEPH.
Eulogy | on | General Washington, | Pronounced in | Person-Hall, | at the | University of North-Carolina, | on the Twenty-Second of February, 1800, | Appointed by the General Government to be Celebrated | throughout the United States. | [*Rule*] | By | the Rev. Joseph Caldwell, A.M. | Prof. Math. at the University. | [*Rule*] | Raleigh: Printed by J. Gales. | [*Rule*] | 1800.
10.5 x 18.5 cm. 34 p. [275]
Not recorded in Margaret B. Stillwell's *Washington Eulogies*, New York, 1916.
NcU.

FREEMASONS. *North Carolina. Grand Lodge.*
Proceedings | of the | Grand Lodge | of | North-Carolina, | For the Year A.L. 5800, A.D. 1800 | [*Filet*] | Raleigh: | Printed by Brothers Hodge & Boylan. | [1800 ?] [276]
13 x 20 cm. 16 p.
NNFM. PPFM.

FREEMASONS. *North Carolina. Grand Lodge.*
To Brother [*name in MS*] | [Raleigh ? 1800 ?] [277]
22 x 35.5 cm. Broadside.
Appointment to visit the lodges on behalf of the Grand Master. The copy described is filled in with the name of "The Hon. Edward Jones" and the date "January, 1800," in MS.
DSC.

HAYWOOD, JOHN.
The | Duty and Office | of | Justices of Peace, | and of | Sheriffs, Coroners, Constables, &c. | According to the Laws of the State of North Carolina. | To which is added | An Appendix, | Containing the Act directing the Mode of recovering Debts | of twenty Pounds and under; the Declaration of Rights | and Constitution of this State; the Constitution of | the United States, | with the Amendments | thereto; and an Abstract from the Act of | Congress, laying Duties on stamped | Vellum, Parchment and Paper. | Together with | A Collection of the most useful Precedents. | [*Rule*] | By John Haywood, Esquire. | Late one of the Judges of the Superior Courts of Law and Equity. | [*Rule*] | Halifax: | Printed by Abraham Hodge. | M.DCCC. [278]
12.5 x 20 cm. viii, 400 p.
Advertised in the *North-Carolina Minerva and Raleigh Advertiser* of December 23, 1800 (notice dated December 20) as "Just published and for sale at this office . . . "
CSmH. NcAS (2 copies). *NcD. NcU. MH. MH-L. RPJCB. Cotten.*

Hodge & Boylan's | North-Carolina | Almanack, | For the Year of our Lord 1801. | Being the first after Bissextile or Leap Year, and the 25th — | 26th of American Independence. | Containing | The Lunations, Rising and Setting of the Sun, | Moon and Seven Stars, Solar and Lunar | Eclipses, Remarkable Days, &c. | Also, | A variety of useful and amusing Articles. | [*Filet*] | Calculated for the state of North-Carolina, being precisely | adapted to the meridian and latitude of the city of Raleigh. | [*Rule*] | By P. B. Teacher of the Mathematicks, | Richmond County, North-Carolina. | [*Rule*] | Halifax: | Printed by Abraham Hodge. | 1800.] [279]
11 x 19 cm. 48 p.
Cotten. MWA.

LORETZ, ANDREW.
[Funeral Sermon on the death of General Washington. Lincolnton? 1800] [280]

According to G. William Welker, "His discourse at Lincolnton on General Washington is still spoken of in that region as one of transcendent ability . . . Judge D. Schenck, in an article in a Lincolnton paper, thus speaks of Mr. Loretz: ' . . . He preached a funeral sermon on the death of General Washington, which was so original and eloquent that it was published in pamphlet and sent through the country.'" *Colonial Records,* VIII: 755-756. Not mentioned in Margaret B. Stillwell's *Washington Eulogies,* New York, 1916.

McCorkle, Samuel Eusebius.
True Greatness. A sermon on the death of Gen. George Washington; the substance of which was delivered at Thyatira on Sunday, January 12th; and afterwards with some additions in Salisbury, February 11, 1800. By Samuel Eusebius M'Corkle . . . Lincolnton; Printed by John M. Slump, at his English and German Printing-Office, 1800. [281]
11.5 x 21.5 cm. 27, [2] p. Title in mourning border.
Weeks no. 128, from Sabin 43097 (not located). Stillwell no. 375.
DLC (but volume reported "lost" in May, 1935).

McRee, James.
An | Eulogium, | or | Funeral Discourse: | Delivered at Salisbury, on the 22nd. February, | 1800; by the Revd. James M'Ree: | In commemoration of the death of | General George Washington. | [*Filet*] | Salisbury: | Printed by Francis Coupee. | 1800. [282]
8.5 x 15 cm. 20 p.
NN (slightly mutilated).

North Carolina. *General Assembly. House of Commons.*
Journal | of the | House of Commons. | [*Rule*] | State of North Carolina. | At a General Assembly begun and held at the City of Raleigh, on Monday, the 18th of November, in the Year of our | Lord one thousand seven hundred and ninety-nine, and of the Independence of the United States of America the 24th: | It being the first Session of this Assembly. | [*Rule*] | [Raleigh: Hodge & Boylan, 1800.] [283]

AN

EULOGIUM,

OR

FUNERAL DISCOURSE;

Delivered at SALISBURY, *on the 22nd. February,*
1800; *by the Revd.* JAMES M'REE ·
IN COMMEMORATION OF THE DEATH OF
GENERAL GEORGE WASHINGTON.

———————

SALISBURY:

PRINTED BY FRANCIS COUPEE.
1800.

21.5 x 37 cm. 68 p.
Caption title. Imprint on p. 68: Raleigh: Printed by Hodge & Boylan, Printers to the State.
The session lasted to December 23, 1799.
Weeks no. 126.
DLC. Nc-Law.

NORTH CAROLINA. *General Assembly. Senate.*
[*Type ornament*] | Journal | of the | Senate. | [*Broken thick-thin rule*] | State of North-Carolina. | At a General Assembly, begun and held at the City of Raleigh, on Monday | the eighteenth day of November, in the year of our Lord one thousand seven | hundred and ninety-nine, and in the twenty-fourth year of the Independence of | the said State. It being the first Session of said Assembly. | [*Broken thin-thick rule*]. | [Raleigh: Hodge & Boylan, 1800.] [284]
20.5 x 27 cm. 60 p.
Caption title; no imprint. The Journal of the House and the Laws of this session were printed by Hodge & Boylan, Raleigh.
Weeks no. 125.
DLC. Nc-Law.

NORTH CAROLINA. *Laws, statutes, etc.*
[*Typographic headband*] | Laws | of | North-Carolina. | [*Thick-thin rule*] | At a General Assembly, begun and held at Raleigh, on the | eighteenth day of November, in the year of our Lord one thousand | seven hundred and ninety-nine, and in the twenty-fourth year of the | Independence of the said State: Being the first Session of the said Assembly. | [*Thin-thick rule*] | [Raleigh: Hodge & Boylan, 1800.] [285]
21 x 32.5 cm. 41, [3] p.
Caption title. Imprint at end: Printed by Hodge & Boylan, Printers to the State. Weeks no. 127.
MH-L. NcU. DLC. NN. NNB. RPL.

NORTH CAROLINA. *Laws, statutes, etc.*
[*Typographic headband*] | Laws | of | North-Carolina. | [*Thick-*

[168]

AN
ORATION
ON THE
Death
OF
General George Washington,

LATE PRESIDENT OF THE UNITED STATES;

DELIVERED IN CHARLOTTE,

February 22, 1800,

TO THE

CITIZENS OF MECKLENBURGH COUNTY,

And published at the Request of

THE MILITIA OFFICERS OF SAID COUNTY.

BY

JAMES WALLIS.

Raleigh:

PRINTED BY JOSEPH GALES.

1800.

thin rule] | At a General Assembly, begun and held at Raleigh, on the | eighteenth day of November, in the year of our Lord one thousand | seven hundred and ninety-nine, and in the twenty-fourth year of the | Independence of the said State: Being the first Session of the said Assembly. | [*Thin-thick rule*] [286]
20 x 32.5 cm. 20 p.
Caption title; no imprint.
A supplement to Iredell's Revision.
MH-L. NcU (2 copies).

NORTH CAROLINA. *Laws, statutes, etc.*
[*Typographic headband*] | Index | to the | Appendix. | [*Short rule*] | [Raleigh: Hodge & Boylan, 1800?] [287]
20 x 32. cm. 8 p.
Caption title; no imprint.
A supplement to Iredell's Revision.
Weeks 1896, p. 265, refers to "An index to the appendices through 1798." In the collated volumes this 8-page index follows the laws of December, 1799.
MH-L. NcU.

NORTH CAROLINA. *University.*
Laws | of the | University | of | North-Carolina; | Established by the | Board of Trustees, | at their Session in December, | 1799. | [*Rule*] | Raleigh: | Printed By J. Gales. | [*Rule*] | 1800. [288]
10.5 x 17 cm. 24 p.
Weeks 1896, p. 267, no. 132.
NcU.

UNITED STATES. *Laws, statutes, etc.*
Acts passed at the First Session of the Sixth Congress | of the | United States, | Begun and held at the city of Philadelphia, in the state of Pennsylvania, on Monday the second of December, 1799. | [Halifax: Abraham Hodge. 1800] [289]
24.5 x 36 cm. 28 p.
Title, as above, printed in the center of the page. At the bottom of the page

is the line: No. 1. Supplement to the North-Carolina Journal, No. 409.—
Halifax: Printed by A. Hodge. (No. 409 of the *North-Carolina Journal*
was dated May 19, 1800.)
MH-L.

WALLIS, JAMES.
An | Oration | on the | Death | of | General Washington, | late
President of the United States; | delivered in Charlotte, | February 22, 1800, | to the | citizens of Mecklenburgh County, | And
published at the Request of | the militia officers of said county. |
[*Ornament*] | By | James Wallis. | [*Filet*] | Raleigh: | Printed
by Joseph Gales. | [*Short rule*] | 1800   [290]
12 x 20 cm. 16 p.
NN.

AN ADDENDUM

Too late for inclusion in the body of this bibliography, there were received descriptions of three rare North Carolina imprints relating to the federal constitution which are in the collection of Mr. Matt B. Jones, of Newton Center, Mass.

One of these rarities has been described as No. 132 in the bibliography. A second has been listed as No. 133, but with no copy located. The third is entirely new. Descriptions of No. 133 and of the previously unknown imprint are as follows:

[IREDELL, JAMES, *and* ARCHIBALD MACLAINE]
Answers | to | Mr. Mason's Objections | to the | New Constitution | Recommended by the late Convention at Philadelphia. | [*Filet*] | To which is added, | An Address | To the Freemen of North-Carolina. | By Publicola. | [*Thin-thick-thin rule*] | [Newbern: Printed by Hodge and Wills. 1788.]   [133]

21 x 35 cm. 12 p. Text in 2 columns.
Caption title. Imprint on p. 12: Newbern: Printed by Hodge and Wills. The "Answers to Mr. Mason's Objections" ends at the top of the first column on p. 10, over the name "Marcus" with the date "January 1788." The address "To the Freemen of the state of North-Carolina" which fol-

lows is over the name "Publicola" without date. See the note on no. 133 in the body of the bibliography.
Collection of Matt B. Jones.

[IREDELL, JAMES?]
To the People of the State of | North-Carolina. | Friends and Fellow Citizens, | [*At end*:] A Citizen of North-Carolina. | August 18, 1788. | [Newborn? Hodge & Wills? 1788.]   [133a]

21.5 x 36.5 cm. 3 p.
Caption title; no imprint.
Contains a vigorous protest against the failure of the North Carolina convention to ratify the federal constitution. Letters to James Iredell from William R. Davie, Archibald Maclaine, and John Swann (McRee, *Life and Correspondence of James Iredell,* p. 239-240) indicate that by August, 1788, Iredell had prepared an address or argument on the failure of ratification. This title may be the address referred to.
Collection of Matt B. Jones.

    Necessarily, because of its receipt when the earlier pages were already in press, none of the material in this addendum is represented in the summaries in the introduction, in the bibliography itself, or in the indexes to this volume. I desire to express to Mr. Jones my appreciation for his courtesy in providing me with photostats on which these descriptions are based.

D. C. McM.

February 7, 1939.

DOUBTFUL TITLES

THE titles listed below are of questionable validity as North Carolina imprints, since the sources from which they are taken do not provide satisfactory evidence that they were actually printed in North Carolina, or that they were ever printed at all.

Of these doubtful titles, 27 are based solely on the *American Bibliography* of Charles Evans, unsupported by any contemporary evidence of publication, such as advertisements in North Carolina or other newspapers. Most of these are minutes of Baptist associations, the printing of which Evans may have assumed from John Asplund's *Universal Register of the Baptist Denomination in North America* (Boston, 1794). It is quite evident that Evans never saw copies of these minutes, yet to many of their titles he added places of printing and names of printers.

Three of the 27 titles found only in Evans are recorded from copyright entries. These titles, though copyrighted, may never have been printed and distributed. Early copyright entries, which were sometimes made while works were still in manuscript, or even in contemplation, provide clues, of course, to titles to be sought for but do not of themselves constitute sufficient evidence of actual publication.

Four more of the titles following are also listed by Evans, but are also supported by newspaper advertisements or other evidence. The evidence, however, is not sufficient to justify a conclusion that the works were actually printed or that, if printed, they were printed in North Carolina.

It should be noted here that three titles which have been included in the main list rest solely on the authority of Evans. These are nos. 100 (Evans 15945, from which Weeks took his no. 45), 119 (Evans 18821, Weeks 60), and 228 (Evans 31472, followed by Sabin 91442). The feeling which led to their inclusion among the valid North Carolina imprints is admittedly largely subjective on the part of the compiler; perhaps they would better have been included among the doubtful titles.

SMITH, MICHAEL.   1756

A sermon preached before the Honourable House of Assembly in North Carolina, October 6, 1756. By Michael Smith, A. B. Newbern: Printed by James Davis. 1756. 8vo.   [D 1]

Listed by Sabin 83613 as "a factitious title," citing the journals of the assembly. In the journal of the Council (upper house), under the date of Friday, 8th October, 1756, is the following: "Resolved that the thanks of this House be given to the Revnd. Mr. Michael Smith for his sermon preached before his Excellency the Governor and both Houses of the General Assembly on the sixth of October instant being a day appointed for a solemn fast, and that he be desired to publish the same." (*Colonial Records*, v, 665.) In the journal of the House of Assembly, under the date of Thursday, October 7th, 1756, is the following: "On motion resolved that Mr. Barker and Mr. Ormond return the Thanks of the House to the Reverend Mr. Smith for his Sermon preached before the House yesterday and to desire a Copy thereof in Order to have the same printed." And on Friday, October 8th, 1765: "Mr. Ormond acquainted the House that . . . Mr. Barker and himself had waited on the Reverend Mr. Smith and had returned him the Thanks of the House for the Sermon Preached before the Assembly on Wednesday last and obtained a Copy thereof which he delivered in at the Table. Ordered the same be Printed." (*Colonial Records*, v, 696.) No other mention of this sermon has been found.

1774

NORTH CAROLINA. *Provincial Congress.*
Journal of the Convention which met in Newbern in August, 1774. [D 2]
Title from Weeks no. 36, with the note "Col. Wm. L. Saunders, Secretary of State, tells me that there is a printed copy of this Journal in his office." In reply to an inquiry to the North Carolina Historical Commission, Mr. A. R. Newsome, secretary of the commission, wrote on January 12, 1935: "I have not found the journal of the First Provincial Congress, August, 1774. I note that Weeks did not see it, and that Saunders' report to him was based on recollection. He may have been mistaken, or, of course, that pamphlet may have disappeared in some way from the Secretary of State's office prior to the time, several years later, when the old records in the Secretary of State's office were transferred to our Commission. I also find, upon inquiry, that the State Library does not possess a copy of this journal."
Evans 13497 records this title, but does not locate a copy.

1775

GREAT BRITAIN. *House of Commons.*
The most interesting Debates in the House of Commons ... [D 3]
Proposals for printing this work by subscription appeared in the *North-Carolina Gazette* of October 6, 1775. It seems likely, however, that it was never printed. The proposals read as follows:
"PROPOSALS, For printing by Subscription, The most interesting Debates in the House of Commons that ever were agitated in that august and venerable Senate, the Speeches and Proceedings on the late Acts of Parliament, that were intended to sap the Foundations of American Freedom and reduce these once happy Regions to a State of Ministerial Vassallage.
"The Proceedings on those Acts of Parliament will be mentioned in Order as they were passed, and consist of the Speeches of Lord Chatham, Lord Camden, Lord Effingham, the young Marquis of Granby, the Bishop of St. Asaph, Governor Johnston, Mr. Wilkes, Mr. Burke, William Temple Luttrell, Mr. Cruger, and others; also the Petition and Remonstrance of the Lord Mayor and City of London.
"To which will be added, The following American Papers that have been published by the Continental, and Provincial Congresses, in Pursuance of passing the above destructive Acts of the British Parliament, viz.

"The Addresses of the first and second Continental Congresses to the King, their Addresses to the People of Canada, to the People of England, and Ireland, and to the People of the Twelve united Colonies of America: Also the Address of the Provincial Congress of Massachusetts-Bay to the People of England, after the Battle of Lexington.

"CONDITIONS. That this Work consists of 160 pages in small Octavo, printed on an elegant Type and American Paper, and delivered to the Subscribers, sewed in Boards, at the small Price of three Shillings and six Pence; or neatly bound at five Shillings.

"Subscriptions are taken at the Printing-Office in Newbern, and Subscription Papers will be sent to the several Counties in this Province.

"To the PUBLIC. This is the first Attempt in this Province to perpetuate the Memory of those noble and venerable Senators who have stood foremost in the grand Struggle for American Liberty; and has been promoted and encouraged by a Number of worthy and patriotic Gentlemen in the Upper Settlements of this province . . . " [*Newspaper mutilated here.*]

1777

NORTH CAROLINA. *Laws, statutes, etc.*
An exact Abridgment of all the Acts of Assembly of this State in Force and Use... [D 4]

Proposals by James Davis for printing this work by subscription appeared in the *North-Carolina Gazette* of July 4, 1777. Weeks no. 41 lists this title but locates no copy. Since some copies of a work of this character would certainly have survived, I believe we are justified in concluding that it was never printed. The proposals read as follows:

"PROPOSALS For printing by Subscription, An exact Abridgment of all the Acts of Assembly of this State in Force and Use, alphabetically digested, down to the Time of publishing the Book.

"Together with An exact Table, Marginal Notes and References, shewing the Time of passing the particular Laws, and the Chapters, as printed at large in the revised Body of Laws of this State.

"CONDITIONS. 1st. That the Book will be printed in large Octavo, On good American Paper, and a beautiful new Type. 2d. That it will contain about 500 Pages, neatly bound, and delivered to the Subscribers at three Dollars each, one of which Dollars to be paid at the Time of subscribing. 3d. That the Work will be put to Press as soon as 300 Subscribers appear.

"To the PUBLIC. The Usefulness of a Work of this Sort must forcibly strike every Person the least conversant with Business as an alphabetical Digest must save the Trouble of turning over a voluminous Folio, and present the Reader with what he wants to know at one View; besides its being more portable, and convenient, for Use. The Subscriber therefore hopes for the Encouragement of the Public to this Undertaking, and assures them of his best Endeavours to make the Performance useful. When the enormous Price to which every Article of Life is now risen is considered, he hopes the Public will not think three Dollars too high, nor the Payment of one of them at the Time of Subscription, unreasonable.

"He begs Leave, as he is now solliciting the Favour of the Public on another Publication, to return them his most sincere Thanks for their great Encouragement to his former Labours, his Revisal of the Laws, and Office of a Justice, having had a rapid Sale, there being but few of them now left on Hand. As he is now detached from the Service of the Public as Printer to the State, in which honourable Service he has laboured Twenty Eight Years, he is quite at Leisure, and if properly encouraged, will publish the Book with all imaginable Expedition.

James Davis

"Subscription Papers are taken in at the Printing Office in Newbern, and Subscription Papers will be sent to the several Counties of the State, of which Public Notice will be given in this Paper."

1778

RUDDIMAN, THOMAS.
The Rudiments of the Latin Tongue: Or a plain and easy Introduction to Latin Grammar. Wherein the principles of the Language are methodically digested both in English and Latin. With useful notes and observations, explaining the terms of Grammar, and further improving its rules. By Tho. Ruddiman, M. A. [D 5]

Advertised in the *North-Carolina Gazette* of August 28, 1778, and in a number of succeeding issues through November, 1778, as "Just published, and to be sold at the Printing Office in Newbern, Price bound, Two Dollars." The fact of the publication of this work is established by this advertisement, but it is quite unlikely that a book of this kind would have been printed by James Davis as his own venture.

No copy of a 1778 American issue of the *Rudiments* has been discovered. The earliest American edition of which definite record has been found is the "New American edition," Philadelphia: Young, Stewart & McCulloch, 1786..

1783

Almanack for the Year of our Lord 1784. [D 6]

See the imprint on the broadside described above as no. 106: "Newbern: Printed by R. Keith, of whom may be had the Almanack for the Year of our Lord 1784." It is not impossible, of course, that the reference is to an almanac that Keith printed, but in the absence of any copy of such an almanac and of any other conclusive evidence that there was one, it seems at least equally possible that the almanac in question was one which Keith imported for local sale.

1789

CAGLIOSTRO, GIUSEPPE BALSAMO.
The Defence of Count Cagliostro before the Parliament of Paris, in the presence of Cardinal Prince de Rohan, the Countess de la Motte, and Miss le Gay d'Oliva, co-accused; against the attorney general accuser. [D 7]

Advertised in the Edenton *State Gazette of North-Carolina* (printed by Hodge & Wills), October 22, 1789, and later. Evans 21724 lists this as printed and sold by Hodge & Wills, Newbern, 1789, though the *State Gazette* had been removed to Edenton in the summer of 1788. No record of any surviving copy of this Cagliostro title has been found.

VILLIERS, R.
The Richmond Garden. A Poem. By R. Villiers, Comedian [D 8]

Advertised in the Edenton *State Gazette of North-Carolina* of April 2, 1789, and succeeding issues as "Just Published, and to be Sold by the Printers hereof, and by Mr. Egan, in Windsor. (Price 3s.)" Evans 21547 is probably correct in supplying the place and date "Richmond, 1788." No copy has been located.

1790

BAPTISTS (PRIMITIVE). *North Carolina. Kehukee Association.*
Minutes of the Kehukee Association, holden at Reedy-Creek in Brunswick County, Virginia, May 15, 1790. [*Colophon*]: Edenton: Printed by Hodge & Wills. [1790.] 4to. 2+ p. [D 9]

Evans 25681. By 1790 the name of this association had been changed to United Baptist Association; see the minutes for 1789, 1791, and 1792, nos. 140, 163, and 175. The title Kehukee Association reappeared in 1796 (no. 215).

BAPTISTS (PRIMITIVE). *North Carolina. Kehukee Association.*
Minutes of the Kehukee Association, holden at Davis's Meetinghouse, Halifax County, North Carolina, October 9, 1790. Edenton: Printed by Hodge & Wills. [1790.] 4to. 2+ p. [D 10]

Evans 25682.

BAPTISTS. *North Carolina. Roanoke District Association.*
Minutes of the Roanoke District Association, met at Whiteoak-Mountain meeting-house, June 12, 1790. Edenton: Printed by Hodge & Wills. 1790. 8vo. 7+ p. [D 11]

Evans 26094. No printed minutes of this association, for this or for any any other year, have been located.

BAPTISTS. *North Carolina. Roanoke District Association.*
Minutes of the Roanoke District Association, met at Mayho-Creek, October 23, 1790. Edenton: Printed by Hodge & Wills. 1790. 8vo. 2+ p. [D 12]

Evans 26095.

BAPTISTS. *North Carolina. Yadkin Association.*
Minutes of the Yadkin Association, convened at Dutchman's Creek, August 28, 1790. Edenton: Printed by Hodge & Wills? 1790. 8vo. 2+ p. [D 13]

Evans 26514. No printed minutes of this association, for this or for any other year, have been located.

1791

BAPTISTS. *North Carolina. Roanoke District Association.*
Minutes of the Roanoke District Association, met at Reedy-Creek, June 11, 1791. Edenton: Printed by Hodge & Wills. 1791. 8vo. 3+ p. [D 14]
    Evans 26096.

BAPTISTS. *North Carolina. Roanoke District Association.*
Minutes of thte Roanoke District Association, met at Catawbo October 8, 1791. Edenton: Printed by Hodge & Wills. 1791. 8vo. 3+ p. [D 15]
    Evans 26097.

BAPTISTS. *North Carolina. Yadkin Association.*
Minutes of the Yadkin Association, met at Lower-Creek meeting-house, Burke, October 28, 1791. Edenton: Printed by Hodge & Wills ? 1791. [D 16]
    Evans 26515.

FREEMASONS. *North Carolina.*
The New Ahiman Rezon... [D 17]
    Proposals for the publication of this work by subscription appeared at New Bern in the *North-Carolina Gazette* of July 16, 1791. The "encouragement" forthcoming was undoubtedly insufficient to justify its printing.

1792

BAPTISTS. *North Carolina. Roanoke District Association.*
Minutes of the Roanoke District Association, met at Straight-Stone Church, April 25, 1792. Edenton: Printed by Hodge & Wills. 1792. 8vo. 2+ p. [D 18]
    Evans 26098.

BAPTISTS. *North Carolina. Roanoke District Association.*
Minutes of the Roanoke District Association met at Mill meeting-house, October 13, 1792. Edenton: Printed by Henry Wills. 1792. 8vo. 2+ p. [D 19]
    Evans 26099. The partnership of Hodge & Wills was not dissolved until February, 1793, Wills thereafter continuing at Edenton.

BAPTISTS. *North Carolina. Sandy Creek Association.*
Minutes of the Sandy-Creek Association, held at Clark's-Creek, Montgomery, October 28, 1792. Fayetteville: Printed by Alexander Martin ? 1792. [D 20]
    Evans 26132. No printed minutes of this association, for this or for any other year, have been located.

BAPTISTS. *North Carolina. Yadkin Association.*
Minutes of the Yadkin Association, convened at Brier-Creek, April 23, 1792. Edenton: Printed by Hodge & Wills ? 1792.
    Evans 26516 [D 21]

MCCORKLE, SAMUEL EUSEBIUS.
A sermon on sacrifices. Halifax: Printed by Abraham Hodge ? 1792. [D 22]
    Evans 24488. The firm of Hodge & Wills was not dissolved until February, 1793, Hodge thereafter continuing at Halifax.

1793

BAPTISTS (PRIMITIVE). *North Carolina. Kehukee Association.*
Minutee of the Kehukee Association, held at Skewarky-Creek, October 12, 1793. Halifax: Printed by Abraham Hodge. 1793. 4to. 2+ p. [D 23]
    Evans 25685.

BAPTISTS. *North Carolina. Roanoke District Association.*
Minutes of the Roanoke District Association, met at Grassey-Creek, May 5, 1793. Edenton: Printed by Henry Wills. 1793. 8vo. 2+ p. [D 24]
    Evans 26100.

BAPTISTS. *North Carolina. Roanoke District Association.*
Minutes of the Roanoke District Association, met at Hart's Chapel, North Carolina, October 19, 1973. Edenton: Printed by Henry Wills. 1793. 4to. 2+ p. [D 25]
    Evans 26101.

BAPTISTS. *North Carolina. Sandy Creek Association.*
Minutes of the Sandy-Creek Association, met at Abbot's-Creek, October 27, 1973. Fayetteville: Printed by Lancelot A. Mullin ? 1793. [D 26]
Evans 26133.

BAPTISTS. *North Carolina. Yadkin Association.*
Minutes of the Yadkin Association, holden at Dutchman's Creek, August 24, 1793. Edenton: Printed by Hodge & Wills ? 1793. [D 27]
Evans 26517. The partnership of Hodge and Wills had been dissolved in February, 1793.

A Calculation, exhibiting in mills, cents, and dollars, the value of gold (as established by Congress) from one grain to a pound. Newbern: Printed by F. X. Martin. 1793. [D 28]
Evans 25250. See no. 227 (a similar title, but 1796).

MORSE, JEDEDIAH.
The American Universal Geography; Or, A view of the Present State of all the Empires, Kingdoms, States, and Republics, in the known world, and the United States of America in particular; in two parts. The First Part treats of Astronomical Geography ... The Second Part Describes at large, and from the latest and best authorities, the present state, in respect to the above mentioned particulars, of the Eastern Continent ... To which are added, An improved catalogue of names of places, and their geographical situation, alphabetically arranged ... The whole comprehending a complete and improved system of modern geography, calculated for Americans. Illustrated with Maps of the countries described. By Jedediah Morse, A. M. Being a new edition of the American Geography, corrected and greatly enlarged. [D 29]
Advertised in the Halifax *North-Carolina Journal* (printed by Abraham Hodge), of August 28, 1793, as "Just published in two large octavo volumes ,and to be sold at this Printing Office." In view of the serious manufacturing difficulties involved in printing the maps and text, it seems hardly

likely that this was printed in North Carolina. Possibly it was the third edition, Dublin, 1792, which Hodge was advertising for sale?

1794

BAPTISTS. *North Carolina. Kehukee Association.*
Minutes of the Kehukee Baptist Association, holden at Sandy-Run, brother Burkitt's meeting house, Bertie County, North Carolina, September, 1794. [Signed by Nathan Mayo and Lemuel Burkitt.] Printed by Abraham Hodge: Halifax. [1794.] 4to. 8 p. [D 30]

Evans 27178. The description of this title is so much more circumstantial than those of other Baptist minutes listed by Evans — even to the number of pages — that it seems to be taken from an actual copy. But Evans does not locate one, nor has any copy been discovered.

BAPTISTS. *North Carolina. Roanoke District Association.*
Minutes of the Roanoke District Association, met at Blue-stone, May 1, 1794. Edenton: Printed by Henry Wills. 1794. 8vo. 2+ p.
Evans 27628. [D 31]

1796

GREEN, JAMES H.
Green's Annual pocket ledger, requisite for the gentlemen, merchants and planters. Newbern: Printed by Francois-X. Martin. 1795. [D 32]

Evans 30509 (from North Carolina District copyright, issued to James H. Green as author, 5 March, 1796).

NORTH CAROLINA. *Laws, statutes, etc.*
A Collection of the Statutes of the Parliament of England in force in the State of North Carolina. Published according to a Resolve of the General Assembly. Newbern: Printed by Francois-X. Martin. 1796. 4to. [D 33]

Evans 30909. The 1792 edition (no. 180) is Evans 24627.

PRICE, JONATHAN, *and* JOHN STROTHER.
A chart of the sea coasts, from Cape Henry to Cape Roman, and of the inlets, sounds and rivers of North-Carolina, to the towns

of Edenton, Washington, Newbern and Wilmington. By Jonathan Price, and John Strother. Newbern: Printed by Francois-X. Martin. 1796. [D 34]

Evans 31046 (from North Carolina District copyright, issued to Jonathan Price and John Strother as authors, 7 March, 1796).

PRICE, JONATHAN, *and* JOHN STROTHER.
A map of the State of North-Carolina, agreeable to its present boundaries. By Jonathan Price, and John Strother. Newbern: Printed by Francois-X. Martin. 1796. [D 35]

Evans 31047 (from North Carolina District copyright, issued to Jonathan Price and John Strother as authors, 9 March, 1796).

1798

HOPKINSON, JOSEPH.
Hail Columbia! happy land. To the tune of the "President's March." Sung by Mr. Fox, at the New Theatre, Philadelphia. Halifax: Printed by A. Hodge. May 21, 1798. [D 36]

Evans 33899 (probably from an advertisement in a Halifax newspaper of the edition of the song which was printed in Philadelphia in 1798).

1799

The North-Carolina Register, and Almanac, for the year of our Lord 1800. Containing some useful extracts from the history, geography, constitution and laws of this state: . . . [D 37]

Advertisements dated Wilmington, February 12, 1799, seen in the *Wilmington Gazette* of March 7, 1799, and in the *North-Carolina Mercury and Salisbury Advertiser* of June 27, 1799, contained proposals for the publication of this work by subscription. It seems unlikely that it ever was printed. The proposals, as given in the Salisbury paper, read as follows:

"For Publication. The North-Carolina Register, and Almanac, For the year of our Lord 1800. Containing some useful extracts from the history, geography, constitution and laws of this state: Observations and directions to masters of vessels and pilots, concerning the navigation of the coast and rivers of North Carolina. Abstract from the constitution and laws of the

United States; and a correct list of the members of both houses of congress: — the executive officers of the federal government — the consuls and ministers of the United States, residing in foreign countries; and their places of abode — the consuls and ministers of foreign governments, residing within the United States; and their places of abode: — the officers and vessels in the navy of the United States: — the members of both houses of the state legislature: — all other officers of the state, from the Governor to the magistrate whether civil, military, or such as have appointments under the general government, in aid of the revenue; including public notaries, inspectors of produce for exportation, trustees and commissioners of public schools, town officers, sealers of weights and measures, branch pilots, &c. Also, the times of holding circuit and district courts of the U. States; and of superior and county courts, in the state. Some account of the incorporated societies by this state, their times of meeting and associations. A brief account of the manner and times of doing business in the custom-houses. Together with rates of custom-house officer's fees — lighterage storage — postage — and duties on tonnage of vessels — on stamp paper, &c. — on wheel carriages — on distilled spirits, the produce of the U. States — on lands — on houses — on negroes — of drawbacks and bounties. And some useful tables on money, time, tide, &c. &c.

"This work will not contain more than 150 nor less than 100 pages 12mo stitched. Price to subscribers will be Fifty Cents, payable on delivery of the copies which will be sent them free of postage, to the care of the person in each county of the state, who is authorised to receive subscriptions.

"Those who subscribe for 100 copies or upward, shall be allowed a deduction of 25 per cent. And if the person so authorised in each county, to receive copies of the Register, for all subscribers in such county, should not receive sufficient number to furnish them, by the 20th day of October next; or if the Register does not contain everything promised in the contents, then such subscribers shall be released from any and every obligation of their signatures.

"The Register is intended to be published annually, with such corrections and additions as time may require, to render it a useful Pocket Companion to all its Patrons. The Editors."

ZANCHIAS, JEROME.
The Doctrine of Absolute Predestination Stated and Asserted:

With a Preliminary Discourse on the Divine Attributes, translated in great measure, from the Latin of Jerome Zanchias.
[D 38]

Advertised in the *North-Carolina Mercury and Salisbury Advertiser* of June 27, 1799, as "for sale at this office." Four other titles mentioned in the same advertisement have been identified (nos. 178, 197, 211, and 216) as publications from the press of F. X. Martin at Newbern, of various dates from 1792 to 1796. This means no more, however, than that the publisher of the Salisbury newspaper had the five titles in stock for sale.

1800

VIRGINIA. *General Assembly.*
Proceedings of the Virginia assembly on the answers of sundry states to their resolutions, passed in December, 1798: (commonly called Mr. Madison's report). To which are prefixed those answers. Raleigh: Printed by Joseph Gales. 1800. [D 39]

Title from Evans' unpublished notes, communicated by the American Antiquarian Society. See no. 273.

THE INDEXES

NOTE: Numbers in *italic* figures refer to the pages in this book. Other numbers are those of the titles in the Bibliography.

Addison, Alexander 273
Allen, Albert H. *24*
Allen, Walter *113*
Almanacs D6
   Hodge's North Carolina Almanack *190, 204, 216, 230, 248, 259*
   Hodge & Boylan's North Carolina Almanack *263, 279*
   North Carolina Almanack *152, 161, 171, 225, 258*
   North Carolina Register D37
American Antiquarian Society *19, 20*
American Baptist Historical Society *19*
American Bibliography 13, 175
American Chronicle of the Times 71
Ancrum, John *77*
Archibald, Robert *241*
Articles of Confederation *94*

Ashe, John B. *131*
Ashe, Samuel *77, 111*
Asplund, John, *Register of the Baptist Denomination 175*
Bank of the United States *227*
Baptism, tract on *29*
Baptists (North Carolina)
   Kehukee (Kehuky) Association *140, 163, 175, 215, 242,* D9, D10, D23, D30
   Neuse Association *189, 202, 260*
   Roanoke District Association D11-12, D14-15, D18-19, D24-25, D31
   Sandy Creek Association D20, D26
   United Baptist Association *140, 163, 175*
   Yadkin Association D13, D16, D21, D27
Baker, Thomas *10*

Biggleston, James 83
Bill of Rights 87
Blackledge, Richard 79
Blount, Jacob 79
Boston Port Act, protests against 72, 76
Boyd, Adam, imprint of 77
Breedlove, J. P. *24*
British colonies, proposed union of 12, 16
Brown, Michael, printing office 250, 264
Bryan, William 79
Burgwin, John 63
Burkitt, Lemuel D30
Cagliostro, Giuseppe Balsamo D7
Caldwell, Joseph 275
Caldwell, Samuel 203
Camp, Rev. Mr. 35
Cape Fear Mercury 76, 86
Cape Fear Union Lodge 126
Carver, Jonathan 154
Caswell, Richard 88, 101, 104, 106, 131, 143
Chatham, Lord 85
Cherokee Indians, treaty with 272
Cherokee lands, settlement of 82
Christ Church, Newbern 21, 143
Churches 8, 21, 29, 143, 203, 205, 206, 231, 239, 250, 251, 252, 253, 264, 281
Clayton, Francis 77
Cleary, Patrick 153
Cogdell, R. 77
Committees of correspondence 75, 76, 77, 78
Congregational Library *19*
Congress, Library of *19*
Union Catalog *24*
Continental Congress 75, 77, 87, 88

Coor, James 79, 131
Corbitt, D. L. *24*
Cotten, Bruce *19, 23*
Coupee, Francis, imprint of *167*
Court of King's Bench 182
Craven, J. 122
Craven County, committee of correspondence 77, 78
Crawford, Dugald 126, 164
Crisis, The 79
Crittendon, Ethel Taylor *24*
Currency, paper 15, 22, 23
Davie, William Richardson 127, 131, 133, 261
Davis, James 9, *10, 11, 12, 18,* 39, 45, 51, 69, 70, 72, 77, 92
imprints of *29, 31, 35, 39, 43, 45, 49, 63, 71, 73, 79, 81*
Davis, Thomas, at Halifax 151
Davis's Revisal 45
Declaration of rights 136, 146
Dickey, Philena A. *24*
Dickson, Joseph 273
Dobbs, Arthur 12, 15, 17, 18, 19, 20, 22, 24, 25, 26, 27, 28, 30, 31, 32, 33, 34, 38, 40
Duke University Libary *19*
Dyche Thomas 95
Eames, Wilberforce 5
Eaton. See Hamiltons vs. Eaton
Edenton, To the People of . . . 132
Edmunds, James 162
Education, sermon on 42
Edwards, Isaac, 72
Ellsworth, C. J. 238
Emery, T. J. 80
Evans, Charles *13, 175*
Farriery, A Concise System of 243
Fonveille, John 79

[190]

France
  treaty with 102
  "wicked and enslaving scheme" of 12
Franklin, Benjamin 16
Freemasons 21, 126, 141, 143, 155, 229, 244, 245, 246, 247, 262, 276, 277, D17
Fries, Adelaide L. 20
Fulham Palace Library 48
Gales, Joseph, imprint of *169*
Gaston, Alex 79
Geography 226, D29
Godfrey, William 47
Gracchus, Tiberius,*pseud.* 116
Great Britain
  Court of King's Bench 182
  House of Commons, debates D3
  statutes of, in force in North Carolina 180, D33
Green, Farnifold 79
Green, James H. D32
Hail, Columbia D36
Halifax, press at 151
Hall, Clement 8
Hall, Enoch *10*
Hall, James, Jr. 203
Halling, Solomon 141, 155
Hamilton, Archibald, & Co. 165
Hamilton, John 165
Hamiltons vs. Eaton 181, 238
Harvard College Libary *19*
Harvard Law School Libary *19*, 22-23
Harvey, John 81
Hatch, Durant 240
Hatch, Edmond 79
Hay, John 116
Hayward, J. 131
Haywood, John 158, 265, 278

Henderson, Richard 82
Heron, Benjamin 56
Hewes, Joseph 88
Hildeburn, C. R. 8
Hillsborough, insurrection at, 1768 55
Hodge, Abraham, imprints of *151, 153*
Hodge & Wills, imprints of *111, 113, 115*
Hodgson, John *9*
Hogg, Robert 77
Holland, James 274
Hooper, A. M. 116
Hooper, William 75, 77
Hopewell Church 203
Hopkinson, Joseph D36
Hopper, William 88
Howe, Robert 77
Hunt, J. 131
Huntington Library *19*
Husbands, Hermon 59, 60
Independent Citizen, The 127
Iredell, James 133, 170
Iredell's Revision 170
  Supplements to 179, 187, 196, 198, 211, 224, 237, 257, 269, 286, 287
James, Eldon R. 22
John Carter Brown Library *19*
Johnson, Thomas 249
Johnston, Governor *9, 5*
Johnston, Jacob 79
Johnston, Samuel 145
Johnston, William 214
Jones, Fred 77
Jones, Willie 131
Justices of the peace 70, 166, 218, 278
Keith, Robert, imprint of 97

[191]

Ketring, Ruth A. 24
Latch, John 182
Latch's Cases 233
Latin grammar D5
Leech, Joseph 79
Loretz, Andrew 279
Low, Samuel 142
McCorkle, Samuel Eusebius 205, 206, 231, 250, 251, 252, 253, 281, D22
McRee, James 282
Maclaine, Archibald 77, 127, 128, 129, 133
Maclean, Alexander 83
Manual Exercise, The 91
Marcus, *pseud.* 133
Marsden, Rufus 10
Martin, Alexander 119, 131
  assumed imprint of D20
Martin, Francois Xavier 143, 166, 180, 182, 214, 217, 218, 232, 233
Martin, Josiah 82, 83, 89
Mason, George, Answer to 133
Masons. See Freemasons
Massachusetts Historical Society 19
Mayo, Nathan D30
Micklejohn, George 55
Military lands 212
Miller, Robert Johnston 264
Monitor, The 156
Moore, James 76, 77
Moore, John 157, 183, 207
Moore, Maurice 46
Moravian Church Archives 20
Morrell, E. 24
Morse, Jedediah D29
Moseley, Edward 10
Mullin, Lancelot A., imprint of D26
Murray, James 22
Nash, Abner 72, 79, 107, 108

Newbern
  Christ Church 21, 143
  committee of correspondence 78
  inhabitants 72
  Saint John's Lodge, 141, 143, 155
  site of first North Carolina press 10
New Providence Church 239
New York Bar Association Library 19
New York Masonic Grand Lodge Library 19
New York Public Library 19
Nichols, L. Nelson 23
Nicholson, Thomas 37
North Carolina
  cavalry regulations 151, 261
  committees of correspondence 75, 76, 77, 78
  comptroller 122
  constitution of 1776 136, 146
  convention, 1775 81
  convention, 1778 134, 135, 144
  convention, 1789 145, 146, 147
  council 52
  court decisions 218, 219, 232, 233, 265
  declaration of rights 136, 146
  18th century imprints of
    distribution 19-20
    subject matter 20-22
  general assembly *15-18*, 123, 124, 129
  governors (colonial)
    Arthur Dobbs 12, 22, 26
    William Tryon 48, 52, 53, 54, 55, 56, 57, 61, 64
    Josiah Martin 82, 83, 89
  governors (state)
    Richard Caswell 101, 104, 106

[192]

Abner Nash 107, 108
Alexander Martin 119
William R. Davie 261
grand jury 64, 111
House of Assembly *13-15,* 38, 39, 43, 47, 54, 58, 65, 66, 67, 68, 73
House of Burgesses *13,* 1, 2, 3, 9, 10, 13, 17
House of Commons 96, 97, 103, 114, 117, 123, 129, 137, 148, 158, 167, 176, 184, 191, 192, 208, 221, 234, 254, 266, 283
introduction of printing in *9-12*
jurisdiction of justices of the peace in 218
law of inheritance in 217
laws (colonial)
 collected 5, 7, 45, 50
 revisals 69
 separate acts 15, 41, 62
 session laws *13-15,* 4, 6, 11, 14, 18, 19, 20, 24, 25, 27, 28, 30, 31, 32, 33, 34, 36, 40, 44, 48, 49, 51, 74
laws (state)
 collected 170, 199, 213, D4
 separate acts 100, 131, 212, 270
 session laws *15-18,* 92, 98, 99, 101, 104-110, 112, 115, 120, 121, 125, 130, 139, 150, 160, 169, 178, 186, 195, 197, 210, 223, 236, 256, 268, 285
provincial congress 84, 90, 93, D2
Senate 118, 123, 129, 138, 149, 159, 168, 177, 185, 193, 194, 209, 222, 235, 255, 267, 284
statutes of England in force in 180, D33
University *19, 22,* 288

North Carolina Historical Commission D2
North Carolina Historical Society 46
North Carolina Supreme Court Library *19*
Park, William *10*
Parma, V. Valta *24*
Parrott, James 82
Pattillo, Henry 226
Pennsylvania, Historical Society of *19*
Petition, A, and Remonstrance to The President 172
Philadelphia, Synod of 86
Pierce, Miss *24*
Pinkney, Mr., printer to the state 92
Pitt, William 85
Politician Outwitted, The 142
Poole, F. O. *23*
Presbyterian Church 86, 162
Presbyterian Historical Society *19*
Presbyterian ministers authorized to solemnize marriages 62
Price, Jonathan 214, D34, D35
Printer to the state, duties and pay of 110, 112, 121, 125
Protestant Episcopal Church 188, 264
Public Record Office *19*
Publicola, *pseud.* 133
Quebec, letter to the inhabitants of 87
Regulators, insurrection of 55, 59, 60
Regulus, *pseud.* 60
Reid, James 42, 62
Rowan, Matthew, 11, 14
Ruddiman, Thomas D5
Rutherford, John 22

[193]

Saint John's Lodge 141, 143, 155
Saint Paul's Parish 8
Saint Thomas' Parish, Bath 29
Salisbury Church 205, 206
Schwegmann, George A., Jr. 24
Sermons 21, 35, 42, 55, 126, 164, 203, 205, 206, 231, 250, 251, 252, 253, 281, D22
Shute, Joseph 240
Smith, Michael 21, D1
Society for the Propagation of the Gospel in Foreign Parts 8, 55, 62
Sondley Library *19*
South Carolina 78
Spaight, Richard Dobbs 131
Spelling book 95
Stamp Act, tract on 46
Steuart, Andrew, imprints of *57, 61*
Stewart, Alexander 29
Strother, John D34, D35
Suga-Creek Church 203
Supreme Council Library *19*
Swann, Samuel *10*
Swann's Revisal 5
Synod of Philadelphia 86
Table, A, for Receiving and Paying Gold 227
Tarborough Convention 188
Taxables, table of 63
Thayer, Rev. John 153
Thomas, William 190, 204, 216, 230, 248, 263
Thornton, Mary 22
Thyatira Church 205, 206, 231, 250, 251, 252, 253, 281

Tryon, William 48, 52, 53, 54, 55, 56, 57, 61, 64
Union Catalog 24
United States
  army regulations 173, 200, 228
  Articles of Confederation 94
  Constitution 144
    defence of 133
    proposed amendments to 145
    ratification of 144, 146, *113*
    revision of 131
  Continental Congress 75, 77, 87, 88
  court decisions 181, 232, 233, 238
  laws 271, 289
  treaties 102, 272
University of North Carolina *19*, 22, 288
Vail, R. W. G. *23*
Vance, John T. *23*
Villiers, R. D8
Virginia resolutions 272, D39
Wake Forest College Library *19*
Wallis, James 239, 290
Walpoole, Edward 182
Washington, George, eulogies on 275, 280, 281, 282, 290
Waters, Willard O. *23*
Watson, Richard 240
Weeks, Stephen B. *12*
Whitehaven Parish 264
Williams, Robert 244
Williamsburg, Va. *10*
Wilmington
  committee of correspondence 76
  inhabitants 75
Winchester, Elhanan 174
Wroth, Lawrence C. *23*
Zanchias, Jerome D38

[194]

INDEX OF PLACE NAMES

Abbot's Creek D26
Bath 6, 29
Bear Creek 175
Beaufort County 29
Bertie County 242, D30
Bluestone D31
Brier Creek D21
Brunswick 83
Brunswick County, Va. D9
Burke County D16
Cape Fear River 89
Caskie Meeting House 242
Catawbo D15
Charlotte 289
Clark's Creek D20
Craven County 72, 76
Duplin County 189
Dutchman's Creek D13, D27
Edenton 28, 132
Fayetteville 126, 129, 147, 148, 156, 158, 167, 191, 219
Flat Swamp 163
Franklin County 260
Glasgow County 202
Grassy Creek D24
Halifax 90, 93, 106, 109, 122, 136, 151, 243
Halifax County 165, D10
Hertford County 215
Hillsborough 84, 97, 108, 112, 114, 117, 135, 144
Hopewell 203
Johnson County 76
Lenoir County 175
Lincolnton 280
Little Contentny 202
Little River 37

Lower Creek D16
Mayho (Mayo) Creek D12
Mecklenburg County 205, 239, 290
Meherrin River 215
Montgomery County D20
Newbern 1, 4, 9, 11, 12, 18, 19, 20, 21, 24, 25, 27, 28, 30, 32, 33, 40, 47, 48, 51, 58, 65, 67, 68, 74, 77, 78, 80, 81, 92, 96, 98, 107, 121, 123, 176, 184, 192, 201, D2
New Providence 239
Perquimans County 81
Pitt County 140, 163
Poplar Spring 260
Raft Swamp 164
Raleigh 208, 223, 234, 247, 254, 266, 283
Reedy Creek, Va. D9, D14
Rowan County 205, 206, 231, 250, 251, 252, 253
Salisbury 205, 206, 231, 253, 281, 282
Sandy Run D30
Skewarky Creek D23
Smithfield 103, 105
Suga Creek 203
Sugar's Creek 205
Swift's Creek 113
Tarborough 137, 138, 188
Thyatira 205, 206, 231, 250, 251, 252, 253, 281
Wake County 110
Whitefield's Meeting House 140
Whitehaven 264
Whiteoak Mountain D11
Wilmington 13, 31, 34, 38, 39, 43, 44, 47, 75, 111

[195]

NORTH CAROLINA PRINTERS, 1749-1800
With the number of titles ascribed to each

	With imprints	Without imprint	No copy located	Total	
Newbern:					
Davis, James					
1749-1780	21	59	19	99	
Keith, Robert					
1783-1784	1		2	3	
Davis, Thomas					
1784	1			1	
Arnett & Hodge					
1786	3			3	
Martin, Francois X.					
1787-1797	13	2	12	27	
Hodge & Blanchard					
1787-1788	2	2		4	
Hodge & Wills					
1788	3		1	4	
Osborn, J. C., & Co.					
1798	1		1	2	
Printer unidentified					
1781-1794		8		8	151
Wilmington:					
Steuart, Andrew					
1764-1765	3			3	
Boyd, Adam					
1774-1775		2	1	3	
Bowen & Howard					
1789	1			1	
Hall, Allmand					
1799	2	2		4	11
Halifax:					
Davis, Thomas					
1782-1784	6			6	
Hodge & Wills					
1792-1797	6	4		10	
Hodge, Abraham					
1793-1800	23	4	3	30	

	With imprints	Without imprint	No copy located	Total	
Printer unidentified					
1799		1		1	47
Fayetteville:					
Hodge & Blanchard					
1787	2			2	
Sibley & Howard					
1798	1		2	3	
Roulstone, George					
1790			2	2	
Howard & Roulstone					
1791			1	1	
Sibley, Howard & Roulstone					
1791			1	1	9
Edenton:					
Hodge & Wills					
1788-1797	23	9	4	36	
Wills, Henry					
1796		1		1	
Printer unidentified					
1788		1		1	38
Hillsborough:					
Ferguson, Robert					
1788	1	1		2	2
Salisbury:					
Coupee, Francis					
1797-1800	4		1	5	
Slump, John Martin					
1798-1799	2			2	
Coupee & Slump					
1798	2			2	
Printer unidentified					
1798		1		1	10
Raleigh:					
Gales, Joseph					
1799-1800	4			4	
Hodge & Boylan					
1799-1800	5	4		9	13

	With imprints	Without imprint	No copy located	Total	
Lincolnton:					
Slump, John Martin					
1800	2			2	
Printer unidentified					
1800			1	1	3
Place and printer unknown		6		6	6
	132	105	53		290

SET BY ADVERTISING TYPOGRAPHERS, INC.
IN LINOTYPE GRANJON WITH LUDLOW
GARAMOND AND DELPHIAN FOR DISPLAY.
TWO HUNDRED COPIES WERE PRINTED IN
FEBRUARY, 1939, BY LOUIS GRAF AT THE
FORTUNE PRESS, ON WORTHY ROXBURGHE
PAPER, & BOUND BY SPINNER BROTHERS.

★

*Typography by Douglas C. McMurtrie
and Ragner H. Johnson*